Python Geospatial Analysis Essentials

Process, analyze, and display geospatial data using Python libraries and related tools

Erik Westra

BIRMINGHAM - MUMBAI

Python Geospatial Analysis Essentials

Copyright © 2015 Packt Publishing

First published: June 2015

Production reference: 1150615

Published by Packt Publishing Ltd.
Livery Place
35 Livery Street
Birmingham B3 2PB, UK.

ISBN 978-1-78217-451-6

www.packtpub.com

Credits

About the Author

Erik Westra has been a professional software developer for over 25 years now, and he has worked almost exclusively in Python for the past decade. Erik's early interest in graphical user interface design led to the development of one of the most advanced urgent courier dispatch systems used by messenger and courier companies worldwide.

In recent years, Erik has been involved in the design and implementation of systems matching seekers and providers of goods and services across a range of geographical areas, as well as real-time messaging and payment systems. This work has included the creation of real-time geocoders and map-based views of constantly changing data. Erik is based in New Zealand, and works for companies worldwide.

Erik is also the author of the titles *Python Geospatial Development* and *Building Mapping Applications with QGIS*, both by Packt Publishing.

About the Reviewers

Min Feng completed his PhD degree in cartography and geographic information systems in 2008 and has been working at the Global Land Cover Facility (GLCF), University of Maryland, Chinese Academy of Sciences (CAS), and Global Resource Information Database (GRID) of the United Nations Environment Programme (UNEP). Dr. Feng has been engaged in global high-resolution land cover and change research and is an expert with high-performance geospatial data processing, geospatial model sharing, and integrated simulation. His work has been published in top-ranking remote sensing and GIS journals. Dr. Feng is familiar with OGC/ISO standards and open source tools and libraries, and is also capable of programming using many languages, including C/C++, Java, Python, R, and IDL. He has also reviewed *Learning QGIS – Second Edition*, *Packt Publishing*.

Eric Hardin works in the defense and aerospace industry as a software engineer with an international research and engineering company. While pursuing a PhD in physics, he used geospatial analysis and process-based modeling to study coastal geomorphology and develop robust storm hazard mapping techniques. In his current role, he has supported the development of weaponeering simulation software as well as software designed to automate the processing of LiDAR and other geospatial data in near-real time. Although opportunities are not as prevalent as in past years, he still gets excited about all things geospatial and finds any excuse to use Python—even when it's a little overkill.

Richard Marsden has over 15 years of professional software development experience. After starting in the fields of geophysics and oil exploration, he has spent the last 12 years running the Winwaed Software Technology LLC independent software vendor. Winwaed specializes in geospatial tools and applications, including web applications, and operates the `http://www.mapping-tools.com` website for tools and add-ins for geospatial products, such as Caliper Maptitude and Microsoft MapPoint.

Richard was also a technical reviewer on *Python Geospatial Development, Packt Publishing*.

Puneet Narula is currently working as a PPC data analyst with Hostelworld.com Limited (`www.hostelworld.com`), Dublin, Ireland, where he analyzes masses of clickstream data from both direct and affiliate sources and provides insights for the digital marketing team. He uses RapidMiner, R, and Python for exploratory and predictive analysis. His areas of expertise are programming in Python and R, machine learning, data analysis, and visualization.

He started his career in banking and finance and then moved to the ever-growing domain of data and analytics.

He earned an MSc in computing (data analytics) from Dublin Institute of Technology, Dublin, Ireland. He has also reviewed *Python Data Analysis, Packt Publishing*.

Ryan Small is a technology generalist based out of Seattle, Washington. He is an active participant in the Cascadia Chapter of OSgeo and a DevOps engineer for ClipCard Inc. Ryan has a passion for solving software and infrastructure problems, especially those with a geospatial angle.

www.PacktPub.com

Support files, eBooks, discount offers, and more

For support files and downloads related to your book, please visit www.PacktPub.com.

Did you know that Packt offers eBook versions of every book published, with PDF and ePub files available? You can upgrade to the eBook version at www.PacktPub.com and as a print book customer, you are entitled to a discount on the eBook copy. Get in touch with us at service@packtpub.com for more details.

At www.PacktPub.com, you can also read a collection of free technical articles, sign up for a range of free newsletters and receive exclusive discounts and offers on Packt books and eBooks.

https://www2.packtpub.com/books/subscription/packtlib

Do you need instant solutions to your IT questions? PacktLib is Packt's online digital book library. Here, you can search, access, and read Packt's entire library of books.

Why subscribe?

- Fully searchable across every book published by Packt
- Copy and paste, print, and bookmark content
- On demand and accessible via a web browser

Free access for Packt account holders

If you have an account with Packt at www.PacktPub.com, you can use this to access PacktLib today and view 9 entirely free books. Simply use your login credentials for immediate access.

Table of Contents

Preface

There are several powerful Python libraries for reading, processing, analyzing, and viewing geospatial data. There are also a number of websites that provide high-quality geospatial data, which you can use freely in your own projects. This data will often be the basis for your analysis, providing the shapes of countries, the positions of cities, the outlines of roads, and so on. Using this data in conjunction with the available geospatial libraries gives you a powerful toolkit for performing your own geospatial analysis using Python.

What this book covers

Chapter 1, *Geospatial Analysis and Techniques*, walks the reader through the process of downloading sample geospatial data, before writing a simple Python program to read and analyze that sample data.

Chapter 2, *Geospatial Data*, focuses on the data used for geospatial analysis: how to obtain it, why good data is important, the different formats that geospatial data can come in, and how to generate your own spatial datasets.

Chapter 3, *Spatial Databases*, provides a brief introduction to creating geospatial databases, how to store data in a spatially-enabled database, and how to perform efficient queries against that data.

Chapter 4, *Creating Maps*, looks at how to use the Mapnik library to produce great-looking maps.

Chapter 5, *Analyzing Geospatial Data*, guides the reader through the process of writing spatial analysis programs using Python. Based on the datasets downloaded in *Chapter 2*, *Geospatial Data*, and using the major Python libraries for geospatial analysis, this chapter uses a recipe-like format to solve a range of typical spatial analysis problems.

Chapter 6, *Building a Complete Geospatial Analysis System*, uses all the various libraries and techniques covered in the earlier chapters to build a complete geospatial analysis system.

What you need for this book

The code examples in this book use Python 2 to analyze geospatial data. Any reasonably powerful computer running Windows, Mac OS X, or Linux will be suitable. You will need to download and install the following software onto your computer:

- Python version 2.7 or later, excluding Python 3.x
- GDAL/OGR version 1.11 or later
- GEOS version 3.4.2 or later
- Shapely version 1.5.7 or later
- PostgreSQL version 9.3 or later
- PostGIS version 2.1.4 or later
- psycopg2 version 2.5 or later
- Mapnik version 2.2 or later
- PROJ version 4.0 or later
- PyProj version 1.9.4 or later
- NetworkX version 1.9.1 or later

Full instructions for downloading, installing, and using these various tools and libraries are included in this book.

Who this book is for

If you are an experienced Python developer wishing to come up to speed with geospatial programming, or have specific spatial programming needs, then this book is for you. While familiarity with installing third-party Python libraries will be an advantage, no prior knowledge of geospatial programming concepts or techniques is required.

Conventions

In this book, you will find a number of text styles that distinguish between different kinds of information. Here are some examples of these styles and an explanation of their meaning.

Code words in text, database table names, folder names, filenames, file extensions, pathnames, dummy URLs, user input, and Twitter handles are shown as follows: "Once you have installed it, you can check that it's working by firing up your Python interpreter and typing `import osgeo.gdal` and then `import osgeo.ogr`."

A block of code is set as follows:

```
import osgeo.ogr
shapefile = osgeo.ogr.Open("TM_WORLD_BORDERS-0.3.shp")
layer = shapefile.GetLayer(0)
for i in range(layer.GetFeatureCount()):
    feature = layer.GetFeature(i)
    feature_name = feature.GetField("NAME")
    geometry = feature.GetGeometryRef()
    geometry_type = geometry.GetGeometryName()
    print i, feature_name, geometry_type
```

When we wish to draw your attention to a particular part of a code block, the relevant lines or items are set in bold:

```
from osgeo import ogr
driver = ogr.GetDriverByName("ESRI Shapefile")
dstFile = driver.CreateDataSource("test-shapefile")
```

Any command-line input or output is written as follows:

```
% python readRaster.py
-500 53081919
-84 1
-83 8
-82 9
-81 17
...
5241 1
5295 1
5300 1
5443 1
```

New terms and **important words** are shown in bold. Words that you see on the screen, for example, in menus or dialog boxes, appear in the text like this: "Clicking on the **Next** button moves you to the next screen."

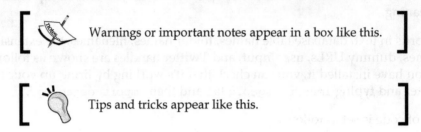

Warnings or important notes appear in a box like this.

Tips and tricks appear like this.

Reader feedback

Feedback from our readers is always welcome. Let us know what you think about this book—what you liked or disliked. Reader feedback is important for us as it helps us develop titles that you will really get the most out of.

To send us general feedback, simply e-mail feedback@packtpub.com, and mention the book's title in the subject of your message.

If there is a topic that you have expertise in and you are interested in either writing or contributing to a book, see our author guide at www.packtpub.com/authors.

Customer support

Now that you are the proud owner of a Packt book, we have a number of things to help you to get the most from your purchase.

Downloading the example code

You can download the example code files from your account at http://www.packtpub.com for all the Packt Publishing books you have purchased. If you purchased this book elsewhere, you can visit http://www.packtpub.com/support and register to have the files e-mailed directly to you.

Errata

Although we have taken every care to ensure the accuracy of our content, mistakes do happen. If you find a mistake in one of our books—maybe a mistake in the text or the code—we would be grateful if you could report this to us. By doing so, you can save other readers from frustration and help us improve subsequent versions of this book. If you find any errata, please report them by visiting http://www.packtpub.com/submit-errata, selecting your book, clicking on the **Errata Submission Form** link, and entering the details of your errata. Once your errata are verified, your submission will be accepted and the errata will be uploaded to our website or added to any list of existing errata under the Errata section of that title.

To view the previously submitted errata, go to https://www.packtpub.com/books/content/support and enter the name of the book in the search field. The required information will appear under the **Errata** section.

Piracy

Piracy of copyrighted material on the Internet is an ongoing problem across all media. At Packt, we take the protection of our copyright and licenses very seriously. If you come across any illegal copies of our works in any form on the Internet, please provide us with the location address or website name immediately so that we can pursue a remedy.

Please contact us at copyright@packtpub.com with a link to the suspected pirated material.

We appreciate your help in protecting our authors and our ability to bring you valuable content.

Questions

If you have a problem with any aspect of this book, you can contact us at questions@packtpub.com, and we will do our best to address the problem.

1
Geospatial Analysis and Techniques

In this introductory chapter, we will start our exploration of geospatial analysis by learning about the types of tasks you will typically be performing, and then look at spatial data and the Python libraries you can use to work with it. We will finish by writing an example program in Python to analyze some geospatial data.

As you work through this chapter, you will:

- Become familiar with the types of problems that geospatial analysis will help to solve
- Understand the various types of geospatial data and some of the important concepts related to location-based data
- Set up your computer to use the third-party libraries you need to start analyzing geospatial data using Python
- Obtain some basic geospatial data to get started
- Learn how to use the GDAL/OGR library to read through a shapefile and extract each feature's attributes and geometry
- Learn how to use Shapely to manipulate and analyze geospatial data
- Write a simple but complete program to identify neighboring countries

Let's start by looking at the types of problems and tasks typically solved using geospatial analysis.

About geospatial analysis

Geospatial analysis is the process of reading, manipulating, and summarizing geospatial data to yield useful and interesting results. A lot of the time, you will be answering questions like the following:

- What is the shortest drivable distance between Sausalito and Palm Springs?
- What is the total length of the border between France and Belgium?
- What is the area of each National Park in New Zealand that borders the ocean?

The answer to these sorts of questions will typically be a number or a list of numbers. Other types of geospatial analysis will involve calculating new sets of geospatial data based on existing data. For example:

- Calculate an elevation profile for USA Route 66 from Los Angeles, CA, to Albuquerque, NM.
- Show me the portion of Brazil north of the equator.
- Highlight the area of Rarotonga likely to be flooded if the ocean rose by 2 meters.

In these cases, you will be generating a new set of geospatial data, which you would typically then display in a chart or on a map.

To perform this sort of analysis, you will need two things: appropriate geospatial analysis tools and suitable geospatial data.

We are going to perform some simple geospatial analysis shortly. Before we do, though, let's take a closer look at the concept of geospatial data.

Understanding geospatial data

Geospatial data is data that positions things on the Earth's surface. This is a deliberately vague definition that encompasses both the idea of location and shape. For example, a database of car accidents may include the latitude and longitude coordinates identifying where each accident occurred, and a file of county outlines would include both the position and shape of each county. Similarly, a GPS recording of a journey would include the position of the traveler over time, tracing out the path they took on their travels.

It is important to realize that geospatial data includes more than just the geospatial information itself. For example, the following outlines are not particularly useful by themselves:

Once you add appropriate **metadata**, however, these outlines make a lot more sense:

Geospatial data, therefore, includes both spatial information (locations and shapes) and non-spatial information (metadata) about each item being described.

Spatial information is usually represented as a series of **coordinates**, for example:

```
location = (-38.136734, 176.252300)
outline = ((-61.686,17.024),(-61.738,16.989),(-61.829,16.996) ...)
```

These numbers won't mean much to you directly, but once you plot these series of coordinates onto a map, the data suddenly becomes comprehensible:

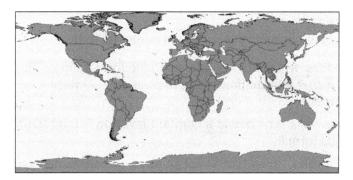

There are two fundamental types of geospatial data:

- **Raster data**: This is geospatial data that divides the world up into **cells** and associates values with each cell. This is very similar to the way that bitmapped images divide an image up into pixels and associate a color with each pixel; for example:

  The value of each cell might represent the color to use when drawing the raster data on a map—this is often done to provide a raster basemap on which other data is drawn—or it might represent other information such as elevation, moisture levels, or soil type.

- **Vector data**: This is geospatial data that consists of a list of **features**. For example, a shapefile containing countries would have one feature for each country. For each feature, the geospatial dataset will have a **geometry**, which is the shape associated with that feature, and any number of attributes containing the metadata for that feature.

  A feature's geometry is just a geometric shape that is positioned on the surface of the earth. This geometric shape is made up of **points**, **lines** (sometimes referred to as **LineStrings**), and **polygons**, or some combination of these three fundamental types:

The typical raster data formats you might encounter include:

- GeoTIFF files, which are basically just TIFF format image files with georeferencing information added to position the image accurately on the earth's surface.

- USGS `.dem` files, which hold a **Digital Elevation Model (DEM)** in a simple ASCII data format.

- `.png`, `.bmp`, and `.jpeg` format image files, with associated georeferencing files to position the images on the surface of the earth.

For vector-format data, you may typically encounter the following formats:

- **Shapefile**: This is an extremely common file format used to store and share geospatial data.

- **WKT (Well-Known Text)**: This is a text-based format often used to convert geometries from one library or data source to another. This is also the format commonly used when retrieving features from a database.

- **WKB (Well-Known Binary)**: This is the binary equivalent of the WKT format, storing geometries as raw binary data rather than text.

- **GML (Geometry Markup Language)**: This is an industry-standard format based on XML, and is often used when communicating with web services.

- **KML (Keyhole Markup Language)**: This is another XML-based format popularized by Google.

- **GeoJSON**: This is a version of JSON designed to store and transmit geometry data.

Because your analysis can only be as good as the data you are analyzing, obtaining and using good-quality geospatial data is critical. Indeed, one of the big challenges in performing geospatial analysis is to get the right data for the job. Fortunately, there are several websites which provide free good-quality geospatial data. But if you're looking for a more obscure set of data, you may have trouble finding it. Of course, you do always have the choice of creating your own data from scratch, though this is an extremely time-consuming process.

We will return to the topic of geospatial data in *Chapter 2*, *Geospatial Data*, where we will examine what makes good geospatial data and how to obtain it.

Setting up your Python installation

To start analyzing geospatial data using Python, we are going to make use of two freely available third-party libraries:

- **GDAL**: The Geospatial Data Abstraction Library makes it easy for you to read and write geospatial data in both vector and raster format.

- **Shapely**: As the name suggests, this is a wonderful library that enables you to perform various calculations on geometric shapes. It also allows you to manipulate shapes, for example, by joining shapes together or by splitting them up into their component pieces.

Let's go ahead and get these two libraries installed into your Python setup so we can start using them right away.

Installing GDAL

GDAL, or more accurately the GDAL/OGR library, is a project by the **Open Source Geospatial Foundation** to provide libraries to read and write geospatial data in a variety of formats. Historically, the name GDAL referred to the library to read and write raster-format data, while OGR referred to the library to access vector-format data. The two libraries have now merged, though the names are still used in the class and function names, so it is important to understand the difference between the two.

A default installation of GDAL/OGR allows you to read raster geospatial data in 100 different formats, and write raster data in 71 different formats. For vector data, GDAL/OGR allows you read data in 42 different formats, and write in 39 different formats. This makes GDAL/OGR an extremely useful tool to access and work with geospatial data.

GDAL/OGR is a C++ library with various bindings to allow you to access it from other languages. After installing it on your computer, you typically use the Python bindings to access the library using your Python interpreter. The following diagram illustrates how these various pieces all fit together:

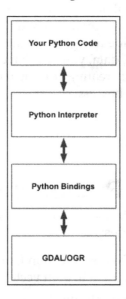

Let's go ahead and install the GDAL/OGR library now. The main website of GDAL (and OGR) can be found at http://gdal.org.

How you install it depends on which operating system your computer is using:

- For MS Windows machines, you can install GDAL/OGR using the FWTools installer, which can be downloaded from http://fwtools.maptools.org.

Alternatively, you can install GDAL/OGR and Shapely using the OSGeo installer, which can be found at `http://trac.osgeo.org/osgeo4w`.

- For Mac OS X, you can download the complete installer for GDAL and OGR from `http://www.kyngchaos.com/software/frameworks`.
- For Linux, you can download the source code to GDAL/OGR from the main GDAL site, and follow the instructions on the site to build it from source. You may also need to install the Python bindings for GDAL and OGR.

Once you have installed it, you can check that it's working by firing up your Python interpreter and typing `import osgeo.gdal` and then `import osgeo.ogr`. If the Python command prompt reappears each time without an error message, then GDAL and OGR were successfully installed and you're all ready to go:

```
>>>import osgeo.gdal
>>>import osgeo.ogr
>>>
```

Installing Shapely

Shapely is a geometry manipulation and analysis library. It is based on the **Geometry Engine, Open Source (GEOS)** library, which implements a wide range of geospatial data manipulations in C++. Shapely provides a Pythonic interface to GEOS, making it easy to use these manipulations directly within your Python programs. The following illustration shows the relationship between your Python code, the Python interpreter, Shapely, and the GEOS library:

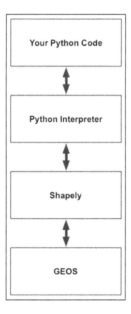

The main website for Shapely can be found at `http://pypi.python.org/pypi/Shapely`.

The website has everything you need, including complete documentation on how to use the library. Note that to install Shapely, you need to download both the Shapely Python package and the underlying GEOS library. The website for the GEOS library can be found at `http://trac.osgeo.org/geos`.

How you go about installing Shapely depends on which operating system your computer is using:

- For MS Windows, you should use one of the prebuilt installers available on the Shapely website. These installers include their own copy of GEOS, so there is nothing else to install.

- For Mac OS X, you should use the prebuilt GEOS framework available at `http://www.kyngchaos.com/software/frameworks`.

 Note that if you install the **GDAL Complete** package from the preceding website, you will already have GEOS installed on your computer.

Once GEOS has been installed, you can install Shapely using `pip`, the Python package manager:

```
pip install shapely
```

If you don't have `pip` installed on your computer, you can install it by following the instructions at `https://pip.pypa.io/en/latest/installing.html`.

- For Linux machines, you can either download the source code from the GEOS website and compile it yourself, or install a suitable RPM or APT package which includes GEOS. Once this has been done, you can use `pip install shapely` to install the Shapely library itself.

Once you have installed it, you can check that the Shapely library is working by running the Python command prompt and typing the following command:

```
>>> import shapely.geos
>>>
```

If you get the Python command prompt again without any errors, as in the preceding example, then Shapely has been installed successfully and you're all set to go.

Obtaining some geospatial data

For this chapter, we will use a simple but still very useful geospatial data file called **World Borders Dataset**. This dataset consists of a single shapefile where each feature within the shapefile represents a country. For each country, the associated geometry object represents the country's outline. Additional attributes contain metadata such as the name of the country, its ISO 3166-1 code, the total land area, its population, and its UN regional classification.

To obtain the World Border Dataset, go to `http://thematicmapping.org/downloads/world_borders.php`.

Scroll down to the **Downloads** section and click on the file to download. Make sure you download the full version and not the simplified one—the file you want will be called `TM_WORLD_BORDERS-0.3.zip`.

Note that the shapefile comes in the form of a ZIP archive. This is because a shapefile consists of multiple files, and it is easier to distribute them if they are stored in a ZIP archive. After downloading the file, double-click on the ZIP archive to decompress it. You will end up with a directory named `TM_WORLD_BORDERS-0.3`. Inside this directory should be the following files:

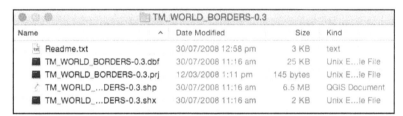

The following table explains these various files and what information they contain:

Filename	Description
`Readme.txt`	This is your typical README file, containing useful information about the shapefile.
`TM_WORLD_BORDERS-0.3.shp`	This file contains the geometry data for each feature.
`TM_WORLD_BORDERS-0.3.shx`	This is an index into the `.shp` file, making it possible to quickly access the geometry for a given feature.
`TM_WORLD_BORDERS-0.3.dbf`	This is a database file holding the various attributes for each feature.
`TM_WORLD_BORDERS-0.3.prj`	This file describes the coordinate system and projection used by the data, as a plain text file.

Place this directory somewhere convenient. We will be using this dataset extensively throughout this book, so you may want to keep a backup copy somewhere.

Unlocking the shapefile

At last, we are ready to start working with some geospatial data. Open up a command line or terminal window and cd into the TM_WORLD_BORDERS-0.3 directory you unzipped earlier. Then type python to fire up your Python interpreter.

We're going to start by loading the OGR library we installed earlier:

```
>>> import osgeo.ogr
```

We next want to open the shapefile using OGR:

```
>>> shapefile = osgeo.ogr.Open("TM_WORLD_BORDERS-0.3.shp")
```

After executing this statement, the shapefile variable will hold an osgeo.ogr. Datasource object representing the geospatial data source we have opened. OGR data sources can support multiple layers of information, even though a shapefile has only a single layer. For this reason, we next need to extract the (one and only) layer from the shapefile:

```
>>>layer = shapefile.GetLayer(0)
```

Let's iterate through the various features within the shapefile, processing each feature in turn. We can do this using the following:

```
>>> for i in range(layer.GetFeatureCount()):
>>>     feature = layer.GetFeature(i)
```

The feature object, an instance of osgeo.ogr.Feature, allows us to access the geometry associated with the feature, along with the feature's attributes. According to the README.txt file, the country's name is stored in an attribute called NAME. Let's extract that name now:

```
>>>     feature_name = feature.GetField("NAME")
```

 Notice that the attribute is in uppercase. Shapefile attributes are case sensitive, so you have to use the exact capitalization to get the right attribute. Using feature.getField("name") would generate an error.

To get a reference to the feature's geometry object, we use the `GetGeometryRef()` method:

```
>>>     geometry = feature.GetGeometryRef()
```

We can do all sorts of things with geometries, but for now, let's just see what type of geometry we've got. We can do this using the `GetGeometryName()` method:

```
>>>>    geometry_type = geometry.GetGeometryName()
```

Finally, let's print out the information we have extracted for this feature:

```
>>>     print i, feature_name, geometry_type
```

Here is the complete mini-program we've written to unlock the contents of the shapefile:

```
import osgeo.ogr
shapefile = osgeo.ogr.Open("TM_WORLD_BORDERS-0.3.shp")
layer = shapefile.GetLayer(0)
for i in range(layer.GetFeatureCount()):
    feature = layer.GetFeature(i)
    feature_name = feature.GetField("NAME")
    geometry = feature.GetGeometryRef()
    geometry_type = geometry.GetGeometryName()
    print i, feature_name, geometry_type
```

If you press **Return** a second time to close off the `for` loop, your program will run, displaying useful information about each country extracted from the shapefile:

```
0 Antigua and Barbuda MULTIPOLYGON
1 Algeria POLYGON
2 Azerbaijan MULTIPOLYGON
3 Albania POLYGON
4 Armenia MULTIPOLYGON
5 Angola MULTIPOLYGON
6 American Samoa MULTIPOLYGON
7 Argentina MULTIPOLYGON
8 Australia MULTIPOLYGON
9 Bahrain MULTIPOLYGON
...
```

Notice that the geometry associated with some countries is a polygon, while for other countries the geometry is a multipolygon. As the name suggests, a multipolygon is simply a collection of polygons. Because the geometry represents the outline of each country, a polygon is used where the country's outline can be represented by a single shape, while a multipolygon is used when the outline has multiple parts. This most commonly happens when a country is made up of multiple islands. For example:

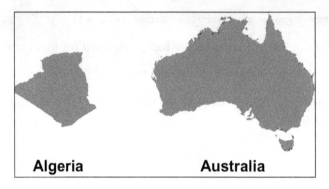

Algeria   **Australia**

As you can see, Algeria is represented by a polygon, while Australia with its outlying islands would be a multipolygon.

Analyzing the data

In the previous section, we obtained an `osgeo.ogr.Geometry` object representing each country's outline. While there are a number of things we can do with this geometry object directly, in this case we'll take the outline and copy it into Shapely so that we can take advantage of Shapely's geospatial analysis capabilities. To do this, we have to export the geometry object out of OGR and import it as a Shapely object. For this, we'll use the WKT format. Still in the Python interpreter, let's grab a single feature's geometry and convert it into a Shapely object:

```
>>> import shapely.wkt
>>> feature = layer.GetFeature(0)
>>> geometry = feature.GetGeometryRef()
>>> wkt = geometry.ExportToWkt()
>>> outline = shapely.wkt.loads(wkt)
```

Because we loaded feature number `0`, we retrieved the outline for Antigua and Barbuda, which would look like the following if we displayed it on a map:

The `outline` variable holds the outline of this country in the form of a Shapely `MultiPolygon` object. We can now use this object to analyze the geometry. Here are a few useful things we can do with a Shapely geometry:

- We can calculate the **centroid**, which is the center-most point in the geometry.
- We can calculate the **bounding box** for the geometry. This is a rectangle defining the northern, southern, eastern, and western edges of the polygon.
- We can calculate the **intersection** between two geometries.
- We can calculate the **difference** between two geometries.

We could also calculate values such as the length and area of each polygon. However, because the World Borders Dataset uses what are called *unprojected coordinates*, the resulting length and area values would be measured in degrees rather than meters or miles. This means that the calculated lengths and areas wouldn't be very useful. We will look at the nature of map projections in the following chapter and find a way to get around this problem so we can calculate meaningful length and area values for polygons. But that's too complex for us to tackle right now.

Let's display the latitude and longitude for our feature's centroid:

```
>>> print outline.centroid.x, outline.centroid.y
-61.791127517 17.2801365868
```

Because Shapely doesn't know which coordinate system the polygon is in, it uses the more generic x and y attributes for a point, rather than talking about latitude and longitude values. Remember that latitude corresponds to a position in the north-south direction, which is the y value, while longitude is a position in the east-west direction, which is the x value.

We can also display the outline's bounding box:

```
>>> print outline.bounds
(-61.891113, 16.989719, -61.666389, 17.724998)
```

In this case, the returned values are the minimum longitude and latitude and the maximum longitude and latitude (that is, min_x, min_y, max_x, max_y).

There's a lot more we can do with Shapely, of course, but this is enough to prove that the Shapely library is working, and that we can read geospatial data from a shapefile and convert it into a Shapely geometry object for analysis.

This is as far as we want to go with using the Python shell directly—the shell is great for quick experiments like this, but it quickly gets tedious having to retype lines (or use the command history) when you make a typo. For anything more serious, you will want to write a Python program. In the final section of this chapter, we'll do exactly that: create a Python program that builds on what we have learned to solve a useful geospatial analysis problem.

A program to identify neighboring countries

For our first real geospatial analysis program, we are going to write a Python script that identifies neighboring countries. The basic concept is to extract the polygon or multipolygon for each country and see which other countries each polygon or multipolygon touches. For each country, we will display a list of other countries that border that country.

Let's start by creating the Python script. Create a new file named borderingCountries.py and place it in the same directory as the TM_WORLD_BORDERS-0.3.shp shapefile you downloaded earlier. Then enter the following into this file:

```python
import osgeo.ogr
import shapely.wkt

def main():
    shapefile = osgeo.ogr.Open("TM_WORLD_BORDERS-0.3.shp")
    layer = shapefile.GetLayer(0)

    countries = {} # Maps country name to Shapely geometry.

    for i in range(layer.GetFeatureCount()):
        feature = layer.GetFeature(i)
        country = feature.GetField("NAME")
        outline = shapely.wkt.loads(feature.GetGeometryRef().ExportToWkt())

        countries[country] = outline

    print "Loaded %d countries" % len(countries)

if __name__ == "__main__":
    main()
```

So far, this is pretty straightforward. We are using the techniques we learned earlier to read the contents of the shapefile into memory and converting each country's geometry into a Shapely object. The results are stored in the countries dictionary. Finally, notice that we've placed the program logic into a function called main() — this is good practice as it lets us use a return statement to handle errors.

Now run your program just to make sure it works:

```
$ python borderingCountries.py
Loaded 246 countries
```

Our next task is to identify the bordering countries. Our basic logic will be to iterate through each country and then find the other countries that border this one. Here is the relevant code, which you should add to the end of your main() function:

```python
    for country in sorted(countries.keys()):
        outline = countries[country]

        for other_country in sorted(countries.keys()):
```

```
        if country == other_country: continue

        other_outline = countries[other_country]

        if outline.touches(other_outline):

            print "%s borders %s" % (country, other_country)
```

As you can see, we use the `touches()` method to check if the two countries' geometries are touching.

Running this program will now show you the countries that border each other:

```
$ python borderingCountries.py
Loaded 246 countries
Afghanistan borders Tajikistan
Afghanistan borders Uzbekistan
Albania borders Montenegro
Albania borders Serbia
Albania borders The former Yugoslav Republic of Macedonia
Algeria borders Libyan Arab Jamahiriya
Algeria borders Mali
Algeria borders Morocco
Algeria borders Niger
Algeria borders Western Sahara
Angola borders Democratic Republic of the Congo
Argentina borders Bolivia
...
```

Congratulations! You have written a simple Python program to analyze country outlines. Of course, there is a lot that could be done to improve and extend this program. For example:

- You could add command-line arguments to let the user specify the name of the shapefile and which attribute to use to display the country name.
- You could add error checking to handle invalid and non-existent shapefiles.
- You could add error checking to handle invalid geometries.
- You could use a spatial database to speed up the process. The program currently takes about a minute to complete, but using a spatial database would speed that up dramatically. If you are dealing with a large amount of spatial data, properly indexed databases are absolutely critical or your program might take weeks to run.

We will look at all these things later in the book.

Summary

In this chapter, we started our exploration of geospatial analysis by looking at the types of problems you would typically have to solve and the types of data that you will be working with. We discovered and installed two major Python libraries to work with geospatial data: GDAL/OGR to read (and write) data, and Shapely to perform geospatial analysis and manipulation. We then downloaded a simple but useful shapefile containing country data, and learned how to use the OGR library to read the contents of that shapefile.

Next, we saw how to convert an OGR geometry object into a Shapely geometry, and then used the Shapely library to analyze and manipulate that geometry. Finally, we created a simple Python program that combines everything we have learned, loading country data into memory and then using Shapely to find countries which border each other.

In the next chapter, we will delve deeper into the topic of geospatial data, learning more about geospatial data types and concepts, as well as exploring some of the major sources of freely available geospatial data. We will also learn why it is important to have good data to work with—and what happens if you don't.

2
Geospatial Data

In this chapter, we will focus on the data used for geospatial analysis. You will learn more about the nature of geospatial data, and discover some of the major websites you can use to obtain geospatial datasets for free. We will then look at the ways in which you can read and write geospatial data using Python.

In particular, this chapter will cover the following topics:

- Why having high quality geospatial data is important
- The various types of geospatial data you are likely to encounter
- Major sources of freely-available geospatial datasets
- How to read and write geospatial data using the GDAL/OGR library
- How to work with Spatial Reference Systems
- Geospatial data errors and how to fix them

Let's start by looking at why having high-quality geospatial data is important.

Geospatial data quality

Imagine that you are writing a program where you need to display the location of each city and town on top of a raster basemap. You dutifully obtain a nice raster datasource to use for the basemap, and then search the Internet for a source of city and town data. You choose the **National Geospatial Intelligence Service (NGIS)** website to download a database of place names, which you then draw onto your map. This database includes, among other things, the latitude and longitude of each place name:

Location	Latitude	Longitude
Abache	7.3551	7.6407
Abacheke	5.50372	6.729519
Abacher	13.816667	20.816667
Abacheri	14.183333	41.5
Abachi	7.3551	7.6407
...and so on		

So far so good, but when your program is complete, the locations look suspiciously regular when the user zooms in on your map:

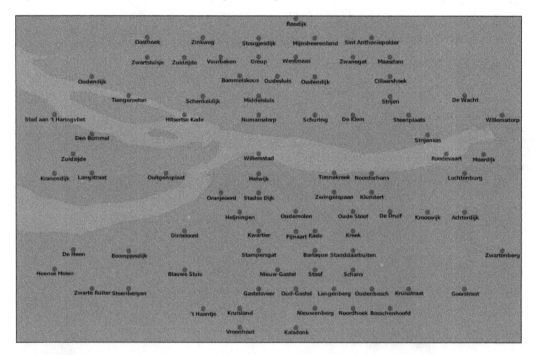

If you were to draw a grid on top of this map, you can see exactly what the problem is:

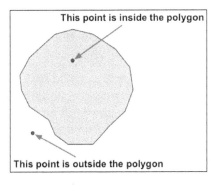

As you can see, the locations are regularly spaced — despite there being lots of precision in the latitude and longitude values, they are actually only accurate to about two decimal places. In the previous image, which shows part of the Netherlands, this can misplace the location by almost a kilometer.

This is just one example of the type of thing that can go wrong if you don't use high-quality geospatial data. Another example often crops up when performing **point-in-polygon** calculations — that is, when attempting to decide if a given point is inside or outside a given polygon:

If the polygon represents, for example, the outline of a country, then you can use a point-in-polygon calculation to see if the given location is inside the country's border. This is often used to **geolocate** a given point (that is, match a point with one or more known locations).

Now, when you attempt to geolocate a point that is close to the edge of the polygon, you can easily end up with geolocation errors if your polygons are not sufficiently detailed:

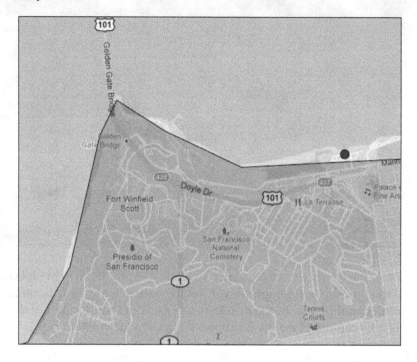

In the preceding image, the dot represents a point to be geolocated. This point is a valid location within San Francisco, but because the polygon is not detailed enough, the point is outside the San Francisco city polygon, and so the geolocation fails.

This problem is particularly acute when using polygons that cover larger areas, such as state or country outlines. Because of the size of the polygon in these cases, precision is often sacrificed.

You might think that the answer to this problem is to have a more detailed polygon—that is, to use more points to make up the polygon's outline so that it more accurately represents the desired outline (in this case, the San Francisco coastline). However, more detail is not always better. The more detailed a polygon is, the longer it will take to process—and if there are too many points, your program might crash because of the excessive amount of data that you are trying to process.

There are ways to solve this problem; for example, by breaking large polygons into smaller pieces, or by **buffering** the polygon to include points close to the edge. But the important thing to realize is that high-quality data does not always mean highly precise data; it means data that is *appropriate* to the purpose you want to use it for.

We will now continue our exploration of geospatial concepts by looking at the various types of geospatial data you are likely to encounter.

Types of geospatial data

In the previous chapter, we looked briefly at some of the more common formats used to store and transfer raster and vector geospatial data. Let's now look at some of the more important types of geospatial data you are likely to encounter.

Shapefiles

As we saw in the previous chapter, a shapefile is a collection of files on disk, which together hold a set of geospatial features along with their attributes and geometries. For example, the following illustration shows the data stored in a typical shapefile:

Feature ID	Geometry	Attributes		
		NAME	POPULATION	AREA
1		Italy	60,769,102	301,336
2		United Kingdom	64,105,654	242,900
3		Iceland	328,170	103,000
4		The Netherlands	16,881,200	41,850
5	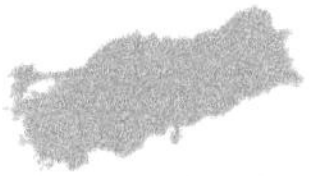	Turkey	76,667,864	783,562
243		Zimbabwe	13,061,239	390,757

Because the shapefile format has been around for many years, and dates back to the dBase days, a single shapefile is made up of several individual files. Typically, these files are combined into a ZIP archive for distribution.

Shapefiles are hugely popular because they make it so easy to store and distribute geospatial data. Practically every GIS system and library that works with geospatial data is able to understand the shapefile format.

Shapefiles, however, do have some disadvantages:

- Unlike almost every other geospatial data format, the names of the attributes within a shapefile are case sensitive. This can cause problems when your code works with data in another format (for example, in a database), but suddenly stops when you attempt to access the attributes within a shapefile.

- All the geometries stored in a single shapefile must be of the same type. This means, for example, that you can't have some features represented by a line while other features are represented by points. More seriously, this causes problems when working with composite geometries such as MultiLines or MultiPolygons, or when attempting to store geometry collections within a shapefile.

- While shapefiles allow you to read through the features sequentially, there is generally no support for spatial indexing. This means that you cannot perform searches based on a feature's position on the Earth's surface. For example, answering questions such as "which countries are within 1,000 km of London?" requires you to check each feature in turn, which is not particularly efficient.

Well-known text

The **well-known text (WKT)** format is not generally used to store geospatial data. Instead, it is used to transfer geometries from one format to another. We saw an example of this in the previous chapter, where we extracted a geometry using the OGR library, and then converted it into WKT so that we could recreate it as a Shapely geometry object.

WKT is a very compact and easy-to-use format. For example, the following WKT string defines a point geometry in the middle of Central Park in New York City:

```
POINT(-73.967344 40.782148)
```

As you can see, the point is represented as an *x* (longitude) value, a single space, and then the *y* (latitude) value. The same general format is used to represent the coordinates of a polygon. For example, the following is a polygon in WKT format, this time defining the approximate outline of Central Park:

```
POLYGON((-73.973057 40.764356, -73.981898 40.768094, -73.958209
40.800621, -73.949282 40.796853, -73.973057 40.764356))
```

Apart from using WKT to transfer data between different systems and libraries, you will also find WKT strings handy when you need to quickly hardwire a geometry into your Python code. For example, the following code shows how you could quickly create a Shapely polygon for testing:

```
p = shapely.wkt.loads("POLYGON((23.4 38.9, 23.5 38.9, 23.5 38.8,
23.4 38.9))")
```

The WKT format is also useful if you want to store geometry data in a text file, for example to temporarily save the output of your analysis to disk so you can load it into another program for further processing.

Well-known binary

The **well-known binary** (**WKB**) format is the binary equivalent of WKT. WKB is generally only used to transfer and store geospatial data within a database. In the WKB format, the coordinates are stored as double-precision floating-point numbers, and numeric codes are used to represent the type of geometry. This format is quicker for a computer to read and write than WKT, though of course the format can't be comprehended easily by a human.

Spatial databases

Just as ordinary databases are used to store large amounts of data and let users make efficient queries against that data, a **spatial database** is a database which is designed to store geometries and perform efficient queries based on each geometry's position in space. For example, you could quickly find all road traffic incidents that occurred within 20 miles of a given point, or find the closest island to your current location.

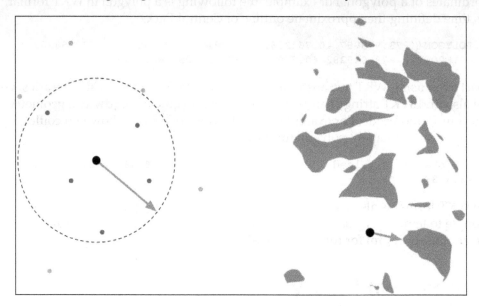

Setting up and using a spatial database is a rather complex task. There are several different types of spatial database available. Among the freely available options, the lightweight **SpatiaLite** database and the powerful-but-complex **PostGIS** database are the most popular choices.

After creating a database, you will have to configure the database to work with spatial data. You will also need to use the database's own syntax to store and query your spatial data—how you do this will vary depending on which database you use.

Regardless of the type of database you are using, attempting to retrieve a spatial geometry will generally return either a WKT format string, or raw binary data in WKB format. You can then convert these into a different format (for example, a Shapely geometry object) for processing.

Of course, with the power available in a spatial database, and particularly the spatial manipulation and query functions built into PostGIS, you may not need to do any spatial analysis beyond what is possible within the database itself. For example, once you have asked the database to identify all the road traffic incidents within a given radius, you would generally just retrieve non-spatial information about each of these incidents. All of the spatial processing is done within the database itself, and once you have found the desired set of records, you would retrieve and work with the results just like you would in a non-spatial database.

We will return to the topic of spatial databases in *Chapter 3*, *Spatial Databases*.

Geospatial microformats

The so-called **geospatial microformats** are typically used by APIs to send and receive geospatial data. Various companies and organizations have defined their own standards for transmitting geospatial data, and so a number of common formats have been developed over time. If you use an API that uses one of these microformats, you will need to become familiar with these data formats.

There are two geospatial microformats that we will look at here: **GeoJSON** and **GML**.

GeoJSON

GeoJSON (`http://geojson.org`) is an open standard used to represent geospatial data structures as **JavaScript Object Notation (JSON)** objects. For example, the following GeoJSON-format string is used to represent a point geometry:

```
{"type": "Point", "coordinates": [-73.967344, 40.782148]}
```

Because GeoJSON is built on top of the JSON standard, you can use the `json` standard Python library to convert between GeoJSON-formatted strings and Python dictionaries. This makes it particularly easy to use GeoJSON in your Python programs.

The GeoJSON standard includes support for the following:

- Representing any standard geometry object (Point, LineString, Polygon, MultiPoint, MultiLineString, MultiPolygon and GeometryCollection) as a GeoJSON string.

- Storing a feature as a GeoJSON string, including the feature's geometry, any number of attributes (called **properties** in GeoJSON), and an optional spatial reference system.

- Using existing XML schemas and processing tools. Because the GML format is based on XML, you can use existing XML parsers and validators to process GML data. You can also create an application-specific XML schema, defining your own extensions to the GML standard, and then use existing XML libraries to work with that schema.

The GeoJSON format is widely supported by software that works with geospatial data. Indeed, the GDAL/OGR library includes support for reading and writing GeoJSON-format data, as does the Mapnik library we will be using later on to generate maps.

GML

Geography Markup Language (GML) is an XML-based format to store geometries and features in textual form. GML is a complex and sophisticated standard. Because it is based on XML, GML-formatted data tends to be quite verbose. For example, the following GML string represents a minimal point geometry:

```
<gml:Point>
    <gml:pos>40.782148 -73.967344</gml:pos>
</gml:Point>
```

GML includes support for the following:

- Representing point, LineString, and polygon geometries.

 Version 3.0 of the GML standard adds support for raster-format data.

- Defining features, and storing attributes for each feature.

- Associating more than one geometry with each feature; for example, a feature may have an outline, a bounding box, and a centroid, all defined as geometries associated with the feature.

- Defining the spatial reference system used by the geometry.

- Profiles that allow you to use a subset of the GML standard for particular sets of data; for example, the GML Simple Features Profile limits the data to representing geometries and their associated properties.

- Using existing XML schemas and processing tools because the GML format is based on XML; for example, you could define an application-specific XML schema defining your own extensions to the GML standard, and then use XML parsers and validators on your GML data.

The GML standard was developed by the **Open Geospatial Consortium (OGC)**, and has now been accepted as an ISO standard. GML is heavily used by the various web standards defined by the OGC, and you will use GML whenever you want to access an API that follows one of these standards, such as the Web Features Service.

Digital elevation models

A **Digital Elevation Model (DEM)** is a fascinating way of representing the curves and contours of the Earth's surface as raster-format data. As we mentioned in the previous chapter, raster-format geospatial data divides the world up into **cells** and associates information with each cell. In a DEM, each cell contains information about the elevation of the Earth's surface at that point. For example, consider the following elevation data, taken from a typical DEM file:

```
2874  2871  2874  2933  2995  3022  3028  3031  3035  3031
2874  2871  2874  2933  2992  3012  3025  3028  3031  3028
2871  2871  2877  2932  2989  3007  3018  3025  3023  3020
2872  2871  2886  2935  2975  2997  3010  3020  3022  3023
2871  2879  2903  2942  2965  2991  3005  3015  3022  3026
2871  2887  2930  2972  2992  2998  3013  3023  3029  3031
2880  2899  2941  2992  3005  3005  3021  3028  3033  3039
2896  2920  2956  3000  3013  3019  3019  3028  3037  3042
2915  2939  2981  3008  3017  3026  3028  3028  3036  3044
2928  2952  2986  3024  3029  3034  3038  3034  3031  3044
2936  2960  3009  3040  3044  3046  3049  3044  3037  3044
2943  2977  3041  3051  3051  3051  3051  3051  3037  3046
2960  3029  3051  3051  3051  3051  3051  3050  3044  3049
```

This data is extracted from a DEM file for Forked Horn Butte, Oregon. Each number measures the elevation above sea level, in feet. If these elevation values are plotted in three dimensions, the shape of the Earth's surface is revealed, as seen here:

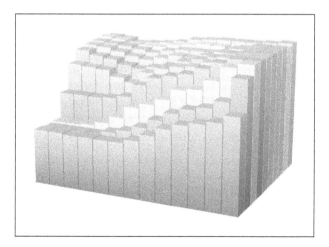

This is only a tiny part of the overall DEM file, but it does show you how DEM files encode the shape of the Earth's surface.

 DEM files also have what is called a **no-data value**. This is a special height value that indicates that there is no elevation value at that point. No-data values are used where you don't want to record or show an elevation value for certain parts of the DEM. For example, a country-specific DEM file would use the no-data value for all areas beyond that country's border.

A digital elevation model is often used as a building-block to construct useful images of the Earth's surface. For example:

- Different colors can be associated with different height bands, using a technique called **color mapping**. If the right set of colors is selected, the result can almost look like a photograph showing different bands of vegetation, bare earth, rock, and snow.

- A **shaded relief** image can be generated from the elevation data. This mimics the effect of having a light source (such as the sun) shine onto the Earth's surface, revealing depth and creating shadows and highlights so that the generated image looks almost like a photograph of the Earth taken from space.

- **Contour lines** can be generated by smoothing the DEM data and running it through a program such as `gdal_contour`, which is provided as part of the GDAL library.

Often, several of these generated images are merged to produce a more realistic-looking effect. These derived images are then used as background maps upon which geospatial data is overlaid.

Raster basemaps

Rather than constructing your images from a DEM file, you can use pre-generated images for your basemaps. These basemaps are often very sophisticated. For example, underwater areas may be drawn using a color map in varying shades of blue to indicate the depth of the water, while the area above sea level is drawn using shaded relief imagery combined with vegetation and elevation-based coloring to produce a realistic-looking effect.

The following image shows a typical basemap of this type:

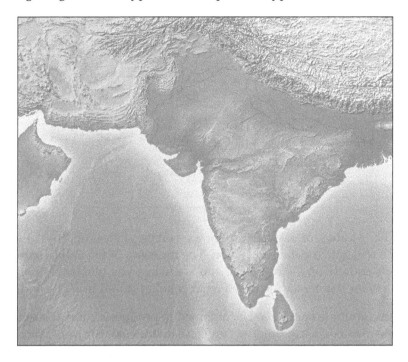

These basemaps are simply image files with associated georeferencing information. The georeferencing information identifies the area of the Earth covered by the basemap. This is often done by specifying the latitude and longitude for the top-left and bottom-right corners of the image. Using these points, it is possible to position the image accurately on the Earth's surface, allowing geospatial data to be drawn in the correct position on top of the basemap, and also allowing the correct part of the basemap to be drawn based on which area of the Earth's surface you wish to display.

Multiband raster files

As mentioned in the previous chapter, raster-format geospatial data can store more than just images. The raster information might consist of values such as the elevation (as we saw earlier in the section on Digital Elevation Models), soil type, average rainfall, population density, and the like.

Raster-format data files are not limited to storing just one piece of information. A single file can hold multiple **bands** of raster data, as shown in the following illustration:

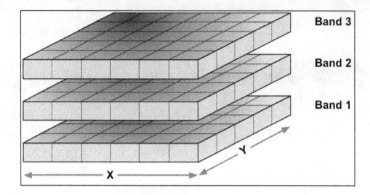

Every band has a value for each cell, so for a given (x, y) location, band 1 will hold a value, band 2 will hold a value, and so on. The meaning of the values stored in each band depends entirely on the raster file you are using; you will need to refer to the documentation for that raster file to see what is being stored in each band.

Sometimes, the multiple bands can be combined to produce a color. For example, you can download raster data captured by Landsat satellites (see http://landsatlook. usgs.gov for details) that includes a red, green and blue color component in three separate bands. Additional bands contain infrared and *panchromatic* values, which can also be useful in certain circumstances.

Sources of freely available geospatial data

Now that you understand the importance of having the appropriate geospatial data and have learned about the major types of data that you will want to use, let's look at some of the places where you can obtain the data you'll need.

There are some situations where you may need to purchase geospatial datasets. One example of this is when looking for ZIP code boundaries in the USA; this information is proprietary to the US Postal Service (USPS), and accurate versions can only be obtained by purchasing a suitable dataset from a vendor licensed by the USPS to sell this data. However, this is the exception: in almost every other case, you can obtain, modify, and use geospatial data for free.

Let's now take a look at some of the major websites you will want to use when looking for geospatial data.

Natural Earth Data

The Natural Earth Data website (`http://naturalearthdata.com`) is a comprehensive source of high-quality and freely available geospatial data. In terms of vector-format data, files are provided in high, medium, and low resolutions. Two different types of vector data are provided:

- **Cultural data**: This includes polygons for country, state or province, urban areas, and park outlines, as well as point and LineString data for populated places, roads, and railways.

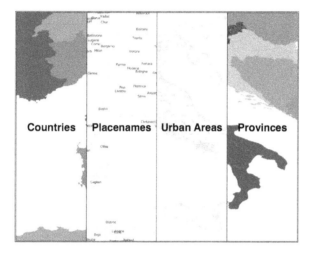

- **Physical data**: This includes polygons and LineStrings for land masses, coastlines, oceans, minor islands, reefs, rivers, and lakes.

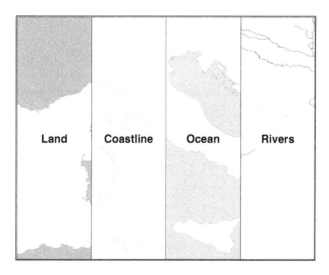

In terms of raster-format data, Natural Earth Data provides five different types of raster basemaps at both 1:10 million and 1:50 million scale.

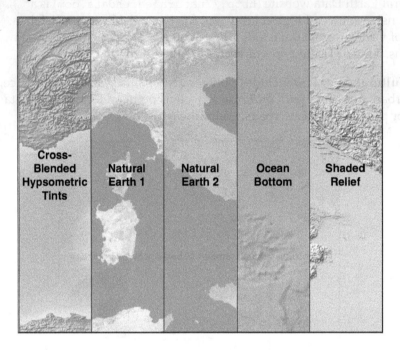

These image files are provided as georeferenced TIFF images, making it easy to use them as raster basemaps in your Python programs.

OpenStreetMap

OpenStreetMap (http://openstreetmap.org) is a huge collaborative effort to create and make available geospatial map data. The website describes it as a "free editable map of the whole world made by people like you". It has positioned itself as a direct competitor to Google Maps. The following image shows part of the street map for the city of Rotorua, New Zealand, based on data from OpenStreetMap:

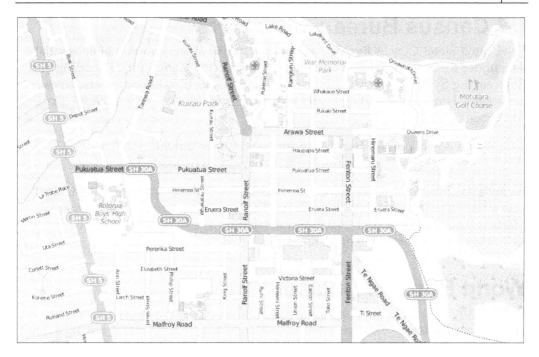

Unfortunately, OpenStreetMap uses its own XML-based format to store geospatial data. If you want, you can download the entire OpenStreetMap database, called `Planet.osm`, and then use a spatial database to access this information. In most cases, however, you will want to use an extract from the OpenStreetMap database, already converted into a more standard format such as a shapefile.

You can find a list of sites that provide OpenStreetMap data extracts at `http://wiki.openstreetmap.org/wiki/Planet.osm#Country_and_area_extracts`.

OpenStreetMap can be very useful if you want to manipulate street maps, or use a street map as the backdrop to display other geospatial data.

US Census Bureau

The United States Census Bureau has made available a large amount of geospatial data under the name **TIGER** (**Topologically Integrated Geographic Encoding and Referencing System**). The TIGER datasets include streets, railways, rivers, lakes, geographic boundaries, and legal and statistical areas, such as states, school districts, and urban boundaries.

TIGER data is available in shapefile format, and can be downloaded from `http://www.census.gov/geo/maps-data/data/tiger.html`.

Because it is produced by the US Government, TIGER data only covers the United States and its protectorates (that is, Puerto Rico, American Samoa, the Northern Mariana Islands, Guam, and the US Virgin Islands). For these areas, however, TIGER is an excellent source of accurate geospatial data.

World Borders Dataset

We used this dataset in the previous chapter. While it is very simple, the World Borders Dataset (`http://thematicmapping.org/downloads/world_borders.php`) provides useful country outlines in the form of a shapefile. The shapefile includes attributes for the name of the country, relevant ISO, FIPS, and UN identification codes, a UN-based region and subregion classification, and the country's population and land area.

The simplicity of the World Borders Dataset makes it an attractive choice for many geospatial applications that need a basic map of the entire world.

GLOBE

The **Global Land One-Kilometer Base Elevation** (**GLOBE**) dataset is an international effort to produce high-quality, medium-resolution DEM data covering the entire world. Each cell within the raster DEM file represents the elevation of a square on the Earth's surface which is 30 arc-seconds of longitude and 30 arc-seconds of latitude. This equates to a square measuring approximately one kilometer on each side.

The main website of the GLOBE project can be found at `http://www.ngdc.noaa.gov/mgg/topo/globe.html`. Note that if you download one of the premade "tiles" covering an area of the Earth's surface, you will also need to download the associated header (`.hdr`) file that georeferences the DEM data. These header files can be downloaded from `http://www.ngdc.noaa.gov/mgg/topo/elev/esri/hdr`.

Since we are going to need some sample DEM data later in this chapter, go ahead and download the E tile now. Then go to the link provided to download the associated header file. You should end up with two files, named `e10g` and `e10g.hdr`.

National Elevation Dataset

The National Elevation Dataset (`http://ned.usgs.gov`) provides high-resolution DEM data for the Continental United States, Alaska, Hawaii, and other US territories. Depending on the area you are looking at, each cell in the DEM dataset corresponds to an area of between 3 and 60 meters square. This is much higher resolution than the 1 kilometer squares used by the GLOBE project.

The National Elevation Dataset is an excellent choice if you want to produce your own shaded relief basemaps for the USA. All the files are available in a variety of formats, including GeoTIFF and ArcGRID, both of which can be processed using GDAL.

Reading and writing geospatial data using Python

Since we will be using the GDAL/OGR library to access geospatial data, let's take a closer look at how you can read and write both vector-format and raster-format data using this library.

Reading vector data

In the previous chapter, we wrote a simple program that reads the features out of a shapefile. Here is a copy of that program:

```
import osgeo.ogr
shapefile = osgeo.ogr.Open("TM_WORLD_BORDERS-0.3.shp")
layer = shapefile.GetLayer(0)
for i in range(layer.GetFeatureCount()):
    feature = layer.GetFeature(i)
    feature_name = feature.GetField("NAME")
    geometry = feature.GetGeometryRef()
    geometry_type = geometry.GetGeometryName()
    print i, feature_name, geometry_type
```

Let's take a closer look at how this program works, and more generally, how to read vector-format data using the OGR library.

When reading geospatial data, the osgeo.ogr.Open() function takes just a single parameter: the name of the dataset to open. The OGR library loops through all of the different drivers it supports until it finds one that is able to read this dataset. The driver then creates a new OGRDataSource object that provides access to the contents of that dataset, and the Open() function returns this object to the caller.

All of this has the effect of setting the shapefile variable to the OGR datasource. The OGR datasource consists of one or more **layers**, each representing a distinct set of data. For example, a **Countries** datasource may have a layer for the country's terrain, a layer containing roads, another layer with the country's city boundaries, another for regional borders, and so on.

Remember that shapefiles can only have a single layer. To represent these different pieces of information using shapefiles, you would have to have a separate shapefile for each of these different pieces of data.

As you can see in the preceding code sample, you use the GetLayer() method to retrieve a layer from the datasource; the returned object is an instance of the OGRLayer class. There is also a handy GetLayerCount() method which returns the number of layers in the datasource.

Each layer has a **spatial reference system** that tells you how to interpret the individual coordinates within the layer, as well as a list of **features** containing the actual data. Don't worry if you don't know what a spatial reference system is; you will learn all about this in the *Dealing with spatial reference systems* section later in this chapter.

We can iterate over the various features within the layer using the GetFeatureCount() and GetFeature() methods. As you might expect, each feature is represented by an instance of the ogr.Feature class.

Each feature has a unique **ID**, which can be retrieved using the GetFID() method, as well as a **geometry** and a list of **attributes**. We retrieve the geometry (an instance of OGRGeometry) using the GetGeometryRef() method, and we can access the feature's attributes using the GetField() method.

Using these various classes and methods, you can iterate over the various features within a vector datasource, retrieving the geometry and attributes (as well as the ID) for each feature in turn. The wonderful thing about all this, though, is that it doesn't matter what format your data is in: you use exactly the same process to read data out of a shapefile as you would use to read it from a spatial database using the OGR library's PostGIS database driver. The OGR library hides all the details of how to read different data formats, and gives you a simple high-level interface to read vector-format data from any datasource.

Writing vector data

Writing geospatial data to a vector-format file is almost as simple as reading it. There are, however, a couple of extra steps you have to take. Let's write a simple Python program that creates a shapefile and then saves some example data into it. This program will teach you all the things you need to know about writing vector-format data using OGR.

Creating a vector-format dataset using OGR involves the following steps:

1. First, we create the destination file by selecting an OGR driver and telling that driver to create the new datasource:

    ```
    from osgeo import ogr
    driver = ogr.GetDriverByName("ESRI Shapefile")
    dstFile = driver.CreateDataSource("test-shapefile")
    ```

2. We then create a **spatial reference** object that defines how the coordinates in the dataset should be interpreted:

    ```
    from osgeo import osr
    spatialReference = osr.SpatialReference()
    spatialReference.SetWellKnownGeogCS("WGS84")
    ```

    As you can see, we use the `osr` module to define a spatial reference, and then set it to the "well-known" spatial reference with the code `WGS84`.

     WGS84 is the standard used for latitude and longitude values. We will look at this in detail in the section on *Dealing with spatial reference systems* later in this chapter.

3. We then add a layer to the destination file to hold the layer's data:

    ```
    layer = dstFile.CreateLayer("layer", spatialReference)
    ```

    As you can see, each layer has its own spatial reference, so we have to pass the spatial reference we defined earlier when we create the layer.

4. The next step is to define the various attributes that the destination file will store for each feature. Let's define a field called NAME:

    ```
    field = ogr.FieldDefn("NAME", ogr.OFTString)
    field.setWidth(100)
    layer.CreateField(field)
    ```

Notice that we define the field name in uppercase. This is because we are writing to a shapefile, which has case-sensitive attribute names and typically defines the attributes in uppercase. Using the uppercase attribute names in shapefiles will help avoid problems later on.

This completes the creation of the file itself. Now let's make up some example data and save it into the file. This involves the following steps:

1. Let's define a simple polygon to represent the feature's geometry. We'll use the WKT format to make this easy:

    ```
    wkt = "POLYGON((23.4 38.9, 23.5 38.9, 23.5 38.8, 23.4
    38.9))"
    polygon = ogr.CreateGeometryFromWkt(wkt)
    ```

2. We next create the OGR `Feature` object that will represent the feature, and set the geometry and attributes as desired:

    ```
    feature = ogr.Feature(layer.GetLayerDefn())
    feature.SetGeometry(polygon)
    feature.SetField("NAME", "My Polygon")
    ```

3. We can then add the feature to the layer:

    ```
    layer.CreateFeature(feature)
    feature.Destroy()
    ```

    Notice the call to `feature.Destroy()`. This may seem odd, but this releases the memory used by the feature, which also happens to write the feature's details into the shapefile.

4. Finally, we close the destination file by calling the `Destroy()` method:

    ```
    dstFile.Destroy()
    ```

    This closes the destination file and makes sure that everything has been saved to disk.

As with reading vector-format data, this code isn't limited to just creating a shapefile. OGR allows you to create geospatial data in many different formats, and you use the same classes and method names no matter what format you are using.

Reading raster data

To read raster-format geospatial data, you use the GDAL library. Let's see how this is done using the DEM data from the E tile we downloaded earlier.

Make sure the `e10g` and `e10g.hdr` files are both in a convenient directory, and then create a Python script in the same directory. We'll start by entering the following in this script:

```
from osgeo import gdal
dem_file = gdal.Open("e10g")
```

As you can see, we use the `gdal.Open()` function to open the raster data file. As we mentioned earlier, a raster datasource can consist of multiple bands of data. To see how many bands there are in the file, you can use `RasterCount`:

```
num_bands = dem_file.RasterCount
```

For this DEM file, there is only one band; we'll get a reference to this band using the `GetRasterBand()` method:

```
band = dem_file.GetRasterBand(1)
```

Note that band numbers start at 1, rather than the usual 0. The result is a `gdal.Band` object. While you can use various methods of the Band class to read the contents of the raster band as raw sequences of bytes, the easiest way to extract the data from the raster band is to convert it into a NumPy array:

```
data = band.ReadAsArray()
```

 NumPy is automatically installed if you use the Mac OS X installer for GDAL. On other platforms, you may need to install it yourself. NumPy can be found at http://numpy.org.

You can then use the NumPy array-handling methods to extract the data from this array. To see how this is done, let's read through the array and calculate a histogram of elevation values from the DEM data:

```
num_rows,num_cols = data.shape

histogram = {} # Maps elevation to number of occurrences of that
elevation.

for row in range(num_rows):
    for col in range(num_cols):
        elevation = int(data[row, col])
```

```
        try:
            histogram[elevation] += 1
        except KeyError:
            histogram[elevation] = 1

    for elevation in sorted(histogram.keys()):
        print elevation, histogram[elevation]
```

As you can see, reading data out of a NumPy array is quite easy.

 There is one small part of our program that may be confusing.
Note that we use:

```
elevation = int(data[row, col])
```

As well as extracting the elevation from the NumPy array, we also
typecast it to an integer. We do this because data is a NumPy
array that returns a numpy.uint16 value for each entry in the
array. NumPy will automatically convert this into an integer as
necessary, but doing this slows our program down. Since these
values are integers already, we simply convert the elevation to a
regular integer right away. This improves the speed of our program
by about an order of magnitude—which is important when you are
dealing with large amounts of data as we are here.

If you run this program, you'll see a list of the unique elevation values and how often
that elevation occurred within the DEM file:

```
% python readRaster.py
-500 53081919
-84 1
-83 8
-82 9
-81 17
...
5241 1
5295 1
5300 1
5443 1
```

Notice the negative elevation values. Most of these are because certain areas of
the USA (for example Death Valley) are below sea level. However, there is one
elevation value, -500, that is not a real elevation value. This is the **no-data value**
that we mentioned earlier.

You can avoid adding this to the histogram by adding the following highlighted lines to your program:

```
. . .
histogram = {} # maps elevation to number of occurrences of that
elevation.
no_data = int(band.GetNoDataValue())

for row in range(num_rows):
    for col in range(num_cols):
        elevation = int(data[row, col])
        if elevation == no_data: continue
        try:
            . . .
```

Using NumPy in this way, it is relatively straightforward to read through the contents of a raster-format datasource. Let's now see what is involved in writing raster-format data.

Writing raster data

To write raster-format data, we need to generate some sample data, tell GDAL how to georeference each cell within the data to a point on the Earth's surface, and then save the data to disk. Let's work through this one step at a time.

1. We'll start by creating the raster-format data file. We'll use the EHdr format, which is shorthand for an ESRI header-labeled file — this is the same file format we used when we read through the DEM data earlier.

     As usual, GDAL makes it easy to work with different data formats; the same code will work no matter what format you select.

    Here is the code to create the EHdr-format raster data file:

    ```
    from osgeo import gdal
    driver = gdal.GetDriverByName("EHdr")
    dstFile = driver.Create("Example Raster", 180, 360, 1,
    gdal.GDT_Int16)
    ```

    The parameters to the Create() method are the name of the file, the number of cells across and down, the number of raster bands, and the type of data to store in each cell.

2. We next need to tell GDAL which spatial reference system to use for the file. In this case, we'll use the same WGS84 reference system we encountered earlier; if you remember, this means that our coordinates are made up of latitude and longitude values. Here is the relevant code:

```
from osgeo import osr

spatialReference = osr.SpatialReference()
spatialReference.SetWellKnownGeogCS("WGS84")

dstFile.SetProjection(spatialReference.ExportToWkt())
```

3. We'll next need to georeference the raster data onto the surface of the Earth. This is done using a **georeferencing transform**. There are many options you can use when defining a georeferencing transform, allowing you to do sophisticated things such as flipping the raster data or rotating it. In this case, however, all we need to do is tell GDAL where the top-left cell should be positioned, and how large each cell is going to be:

```
originX    = -180
originY    = 90
cellWidth  = 0.25
cellHeight = 0.25

geoTransform = [originX, cellWidth, 0, originY, 0, -cellHeight]
dstFile.SetGeoTransform(geoTransform)
```

In this example code, we have set the top-left cell to be at latitude=90, longitude=-180, and have defined each cell to cover 1/4 of a degree of latitude and longitude.

4. We're now ready to create our raster-format data and save it to the file. Let's generate an array of 360 rows and 180 columns, where each value is a random number between 1 and 100:

```
import random

data = []
for row in range(360):
    row_data = []
    for col in range(180):
        row_data.append(random.randint(1, 100))
    data.append(row_data)
```

We can then convert this array into a NumPy array, where each entry in the array is a 16-bit signed integer:

```
import numpy
array = numpy.array(data, dtype=numpy.int16)
```

This data can then be saved into the file:

```
band.WriteArray(array)
```

5. Finally, let's define a no-data value, and close the file to save everything to disk:

```
band.SetNoDataValue(-500)
del dstFile
```

Running this program will create a new raster-format file on disk, complete with a header (.hdr) file and information about how to georeference our (random) data onto the surface of the Earth. Except for the addition of a spatial reference system and a georeferencing transform, the process of writing geospatial data is almost as simple as reading it.

> You can actually use both a spatial reference system and a geotransform when reading raster data from a file too — we just skipped that step to keep it simple. Later on, when we want to position cells exactly onto a point on the Earth's surface, we'll use both of these concepts while reading raster-format data.

Dealing with spatial reference systems

One of the things that can be quite confusing when you start working with geospatial data is the notion of a **spatial reference system**. Imagine that you're running a search-and-rescue operation, and are given the location of a plane crash as a coordinate, for example:

```
(-114.93, 12.478)
```

What do these numbers mean? Are these values a latitude and longitude, or are they perhaps a number of kilometers away from a given reference point? Without understanding how these coordinates translate to a point on the Earth's surface, you'd have no way of knowing where to send your rescuers.

> Spatial reference systems are sometimes referred to as coordinate reference systems. Don't worry: these two terms refer to the same thing.

To understand the concept of spatial reference systems, you first need to learn a bit about mapping theory. Maps are an attempt to draw the three-dimensional surface of the Earth on a two-dimensional Cartesian plane:

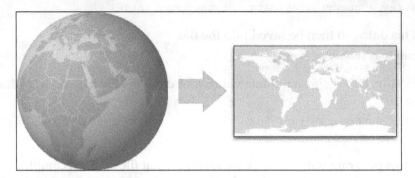

To convert the Earth's surface into a two-dimensional plane, you need to use a mathematical process known as **projection**. The thing is, it is mathematically impossible to have a perfect projection: shapes are going to be distorted, areas will be misrepresented, or the distance between points will be incorrect.

Because of this imperfection, a large number of different map projections have been developed over the years. Some map projections are quite accurate for certain areas of the world, but are inaccurate elsewhere. Other map projections preserve the shape of the continents while misrepresenting distance and areas, and so on.

Whenever you work with geospatial data, you will need to have answers to the following three questions:

- Which mathematical model has been used to define the shape of the Earth?
- Have the coordinates been projected onto a map?
- If so, what projection has been used?

Knowing the answers to these three questions will allow you to know the exact location that a given set of coordinates refers to. As you can imagine, knowing the answers to these questions is vital to the success of any geospatial analysis.

A spatial reference system encapsulates the answers to these three questions. Let's take a look at a couple of common spatial reference systems to see how they work.

WGS84

WGS84 stands for World Geodetic System 1984, and is a global standard used to represent points on the surface of the Earth. It uses an accurate mathematical model of the Earth's shape, along with standards that define coordinates in terms of what we call latitude and longitude. Taken together, the WGS84 spatial reference system provides a complete system to describe points on the Earth's surface.

Let's take a closer look at how WGS84 defines the latitude and longitude values. Given a point on the Earth's surface, the latitude and longitude are calculated by drawing an imaginary line from the center of the Earth out to the desired point:

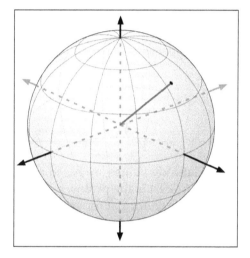

You can then measure the latitude as the angle in the north-south direction between this line and a line going out to the equator:

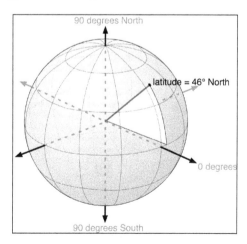

Similarly, the longitude can be calculated as the angle between this line in the east-west direction and a line going out to zero degrees (which is based on the location of Greenwich, England):

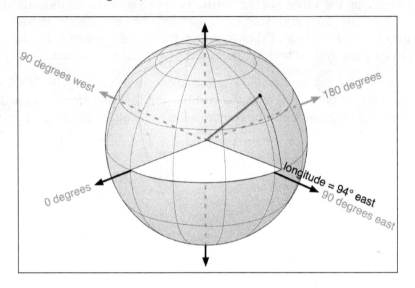

As you can see, longitude and latitude values are based on the desired point's position on the Earth's surface. WGS84 is the prototypical example of an **unprojected** coordinate system. It's a very common format for geospatial data, and in many cases you will only be working with data in this format.

Universal Transverse Mercator

Universal Transverse Mercator (UTM) is a very common standard used to represent coordinates on a flat Cartesian plane. UTM is not a single map projection, but is rather a sequence of sixty different projections called **zones**, where each zone covers a narrow slice of the Earth's surface:

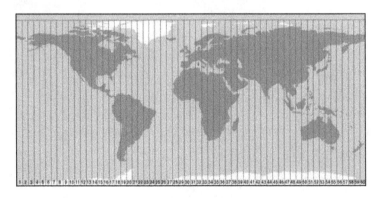

For any given UTM zone, the coordinates are measured as "northing" and "easting" values, which correspond to the number of meters north or east of a given reference point. The reference point is calculated so that the northing and easting values will always be positive.

Because the UTM projections are based on a two-dimensional map, these are examples of a **projected** coordinate system.

Describing spatial reference systems

Whenever you work with geospatial data, you need to know which spatial reference system you are using. Often, when generating maps or reading and writing geospatial data, you will need to build an `osr.SpatialReference` object or its equivalent to describe the spatial reference system you are using.

One of the easiest ways to describe a spatial reference system is by name. We saw this earlier when we created a spatial reference object using the well-known name, like this:

```
spatialReference = osr.SpatialReference()
spatialReference.SetWellKnownGeogCS("WGS84")
```

Another common way to describe a spatial reference system is to use the **EPSG** code. EPSG is a standards body that maintains a database of all known spatial reference systems, and assigns a unique numeric code to each one. You can find the EPSG website at `http://www.epsg-registry.org`. For example, the EPSG code for WGS84 is 4326, so you could also create a WGS84 spatial reference object using the following Python code:

```
spatialReference = osr.SpatialReference()
spatialReference.ImportFromEPSG(4326)
```

Finally, you can use the WKT format string to define a spatial reference system. The GDAL/OGR library makes it easy to import and export spatial reference systems using WKT. For example:

```
>>> spatialReference = osr.SpatialReference()
>>> spatialReference.ImportFromEPSG(4326)
>>> print spatialReference.ExportToWkt()
GEOGCS["WGS 84",DATUM["WGS_1984",SPHEROID["WGS
84",6378137,298.257223563,AUTHORITY["EPSG","7030"]],AUTHORITY["EPSG",
"6326"]],PRIMEM["Greenwich",0,AUTHORITY["EPSG","8901"]],UNIT["degree"
,0.0174532925199433,AUTHORITY["EPSG","9122"]],AUTHORITY["EPSG","4326"
]]
```

There is also an `ImportFromWkt()` method, which lets you define a spatial reference object using a WKT definition string.

Transforming coordinates

As well as knowing which spatial reference system you are using, it is also important at times to be able to transform geospatial data from one spatial reference system to another. For example, if you want to use Shapely to calculate the intersection between two polygons, and the polygons use different spatial reference systems, you are going to need to convert them into the same spatial reference system before the intersection will work.

 Remember that Shapely is a *geometry* manipulation library. It doesn't know about spatial reference systems, so you need to deal with this yourself.

To transform a geometry from one spatial reference system to another, you can use the `osr.CoordinateTransformation` class. Let's see how this is done:

```
src_spatialReference = osr.SpatialReference()
src_spatialReference.SetWellKnownGeogCS("WGS84")

dst_spatialReference = osr.SpatialReference()
dst_spatialReference.SetUTM(10)

transform = osr.CoordinateTransformation(src_spatialReference,
dst_spatialReference)

geometry.Transform(transform)
```

You first define the two spatial reference systems, and then create the coordinate transformation to convert from one to the other. Then you can simply call the `Transform()` method to convert the geometry from the source spatial reference system into the destination spatial reference system.

Calculating lengths and areas

Now that we understand the basics of spatial reference systems and how to transform data from one spatial reference system to another, we can finally solve the problem we encountered in *Chapter 1, Geospatial Analysis and Techniques*. If you remember, while looking at the calculations we could do with the Shapely library, we found that we could not accurately calculate lengths and areas for geospatial data that used longitude and latitude values.

Let's take another look at this problem, and how we can use coordinate transformations to solve these problems.

Let's define a simple polygon that defines the approximate outline of Central Park in New York:

```
import shapely.wkt
wkt = "POLYGON((-73.973057 40.764356, -73.981898 40.768094, -
73.958209 40.800621, -73.949282 40.796853, -73.973057 40.764356))"
outline = shapely.wkt.loads(wkt)
```

We used this polygon as an example in the section on well-known text earlier in this chapter.

If we were to ask Shapely to calculate the area of this geometry, it would calculate the mathematical area covered by this polygon:

```
>>> print outline.area
0.000377902804
```

Unfortunately, the resulting number is in "square degrees", which is a meaningless number. This is because Shapely doesn't know about map projections—it simply treats each coordinate value as a number. To calculate the area of this polygon in real units, we have to convert from unprojected lat/long coordinates into what is called an "equal area" map projection that measures coordinates in meters. We can then ask Shapely to calculate the area, and the result will be in square meters. Let's see how we can do this using a combination of OGR and Shapely:

1. First off, we create an OGR geometry object using the WKT definition for our outline:

   ```
   from osgeo import ogr
   polygon = ogr.CreateGeometryFromWkt(wkt)
   ```

2. We next need to define a coordinate transformation from WGS84 into a projected coordinate system that uses meters. We will use the **World Mollweide** projection (EPSG code 54009), which is an equal-area projection that is fairly accurate worldwide:

   ```
   from osgeo import osr

   src_spatialReference = osr.SpatialReference()
   src_spatialReference.ImportFromEPSG(4326)

   dst_spatialReference = osr.SpatialReference()
   dst_spatialReference.ImportFromEPSG(54009)
   ```

```
transform = osr.CoordinateTransformation(src_spatialReference,
dst_spatialReference)
```

3. We can then transform the OGR geometry from WGS84 into World Mollweide projection, convert it back into a Shapely geometry, and finally ask Shapely to calculate the polygon's area:

```
polygon.Transform(transform)

outline = shapely.wkt.loads(polygon.ExportToWkt())
print outline.area
```

The result is an accurate figure for the area of Central Park (as accurate as the original polygon outline will allow), measured in square meters. You could then convert this area into square miles or any other unit you wished to use.

In this example, we used an equal-area projection. To accurately calculate lengths, you would have to use an equidistant map projection covering the area of the Earth that you are interested in. Alternatively, you can make use of the PyProj library to calculate distances for unprojected coordinates; we will look at PyProj in detail in *Chapter 5, Analyzing Geospatial Data*.

Geospatial data errors and how to fix them

As you start working with geospatial data, you will soon discover that things don't always work the way you expect them to. OGR may crash when attempting to save a geometry into a shapefile, or Shapely may cause a system error when calculating the intersection of two polygons. While this can be frustrating, there are ways to solve these problems once you understand what causes them.

Geospatial data, and libraries such as GDAL/OGR and Shapely, are based around a mathematical model of how a geometry should be structured. Problems occur when your geospatial data doesn't meet this mathematical ideal. Let's take a look at what a mathematically-correct geometry looks like.

Points

While a coordinate is simply a pair of numbers, the range of acceptable values is limited. Imagine, for example, the following point geometries, which use WGS84 (that is, latitude and longitude coordinates):

```
POINT(-0.076 51.506)
POINT(2.295 48.858)
POINT(37.784 -122.402)
```

These points are supposed to represent the location of the Tower of London, the Eiffel Tower, and the Moscone Center in San Francisco. However, the third Point geometry has been defined incorrectly, by swapping the latitude and longitude. This location has been set to longitude=37.784 and latitude=-122.402. But latitude values can only be in the range -90 to +90, and so this Point geometry is invalid.

Of course, all geometries are made up of coordinates, and so a polygon, for example, might have just one out-of-range coordinate, which could cause your program to crash. When constructing or manipulating geometries, you will sometimes need to add code to check that the coordinates are all valid, and adjust the geometry if necessary.

LineStrings

A LineString geometry consists of a list of coordinates, with a straight line segment drawn from one coordinate to the next:

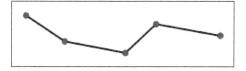

However, if you try to define a LineString with only one coordinate, or a LineString with two coordinates that happen to be the same, then your LineString geometry will be mathematically invalid and can cause your program to crash.

Linear Rings

A Linear Ring is a LineString where the starting and ending points are the same:

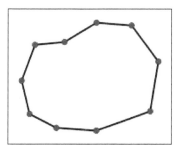

Linear Rings are used to enclose an area of space, and are the building blocks of polygon geometries. For a Linear Ring to be valid, it must have at least three coordinates, and the line segments cannot touch or cross.

The following illustration shows two examples of mathematically invalid Linear Rings:

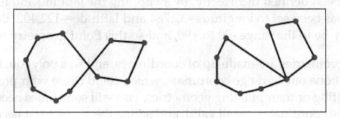

Polygons

A polygon geometry is made up of one or more Linear Rings: the first Linear Ring defines the outline of the Polygon, while additional Linear Rings define holes within the Polygon's interior. For example:

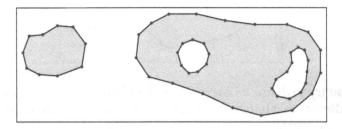

However, this mathematically-ideal representation of a polygon breaks down if the interior rings overlap, touch each other, or touch the polygon's exterior. If any of these things happen, your polygon becomes invalid and your program may well crash.

MultiPolygons

A MultiPolygon geometry, as the name suggests, is a collection of two or more polygons. MultiPolygons are mathematically invalid if two of their polygons touch along an edge—in this case, the two polygons should have been merged into one larger polygon, and so the MultiPolygon is considered to be invalid.

Fixing invalid geometries

Even if your geometry data is valid to start with, geometries can become invalid when you manipulate them. For example, if you attempt to split a polygon in two, or merge LineString geometries together, the result can sometimes be invalid.

Now that you understand the ways in which a geometry can be invalid, let's look at some tricks to fix them. First off, you can ask Shapely if it thinks the geometry is valid or not by checking the `is_valid` attribute:

```
if not geometry.is_valid:
    . . . .
```

Similarly, you can use the `IsValid()` method to check if an OGR geometry object is valid or not:

```
if not geometry.IsValid():
    . . .
```

Unfortunately, these two validity checks are not perfect: sometimes you'll find that a geometry is identified as valid even though it isn't. When this happens, you'll have to add a `try...except` clause to your program to catch a crash, and then try to fix the geometries yourself before trying again.

When a geometry is not valid, your first port of call will be the `buffer(0)` technique. The `buffer()` operation is one which expands a geometry to include all points within a certain distance of the original geometry, for example:

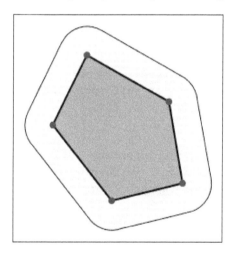

By calling `buffer(0)`, you are telling Shapely (or OGR) to construct a new copy of the geometry that includes all points within a zero distance of the geometry. This effectively rebuilds the geometry from scratch, and will often turn an invalid geometry back into a valid one.

This doesn't always work, unfortunately. There are times when `buffer()` is unable to rebuild a complex geometry without crashing. In that case, you may need to split the geometry into individual pieces, and then check each piece in turn to see if it was the cause of the crash. You can then exclude the misbehaving piece from the geometry when you rebuild it. The following is an example piece of Python code that attempts to repair an invalid Shapely geometry using this technique:

```python
def fix_geometry(geometry):
    buffer_worked = True
    try:
        geometry = geometry.buffer(0)
    except:
        buffer_worked = False

    if buffer_worked:
        return geometry

    polygons = []
    if geometry.geom_type == "Polygon":
        polygons.append(geometry)
    elif geometry.geom_type == "MultiPolygon":
        polygons.extend(geometry.geoms)

    fixed_polygons = []
    for n,polygon in enumerate(polygons):
        if not linear_ring_is_valid(polygon.exterior):
            continue # Unable to fix.

        interiors = []
        for ring in polygon.interiors:
            if linear_ring_is_valid(ring):
                interiors.append(ring)

        fixed_polygon = shapely.geometry.Polygon(polygon.exterior,
                                                 interiors)

        try:
            fixed_polygon = fixed_polygon.buffer(0)
        except:
            continue

        if fixed_polygon.geom_type == "Polygon":
            fixed_polygons.append(fixed_polygon)
```

```
        elif fixed_polygon.geom_type == "MultiPolygon":
            fixed_polygons.extend(fixed_polygon.geoms)

    if len(fixed_polygons) > 0:
        return shapely.geometry.MultiPolygon(fixed_polygons)
    else:
        return None # Unable to fix.

def linear_ring_is_valid(ring):
    points = set() # Set of (x,y) tuples.

    for x,y in ring.coords:
        points.add((x,y))

    if len(points) < 3:
        return False
    else:
        return True
```

 Remember that this code works with Shapely geometries. If you have an OGR geometry, you can convert it into a Shapely geometry using `shapely.wkt.loads(ogrGeometry.ExportToWkt())`.

Summary

In this chapter, we looked more closely at the data used for geospatial analysis. We saw why having high-quality geospatial data is important, the various types of geospatial data you are likely to encounter, and the major websites which provide quality geospatial data for free. We then looked at how to read and write both vector and raster format geospatial data using GDAL and OGR, and learned about spatial reference systems. Finally, we looked at the ways in which geospatial data can become invalid, and how to fix it.

In the next chapter, we will look at spatial databases and how they can be used as a powerful tool for geospatial analysis.

3
Spatial Databases

In this chapter, we will look at how you can use a database to store, analyze, and manipulate geospatial data. While spatial databases can be quite complex, and the process of optimizing spatial queries can be challenging, they can be used in a straightforward way without too much fuss and are an important part of the geospatial analyst's toolkit.

In this chapter, we will:

- Learn the important concepts you'll need to know before using a spatial database
- Install the PostgreSQL relational database system onto your computer
- Install the PostGIS extension to PostgreSQL to support spatial databases
- Install the `psycopg2` database adapter to allow you to access Postgres from your Python programs
- Learn how to create a spatial database using PostGIS
- Discover how to import data into your spatial database using Python
- Learn how to query your spatial database using Python code
- See how you can manipulate your spatial data from Python
- Learn how to export data out of a spatial database

Let's start by looking at the concept of spatial databases and how they work.

Spatial database concepts

As mentioned in the previous chapter, spatial databases are databases which can store and query spatial data. Each record in a spatially-enabled database table has one or more **geometry fields** which position that record somewhere on the Earth's surface. How the geometry field(s) are used will depend on what type of information you are storing in the database table. For example:

- A record representing a delivery vehicle might include a Point geometry reflecting the vehicle's current location.

- A record representing a road might include a LineString geometry representing the shape of the road.

- A record representing a forest fire might include a Polygon geometry representing the area affected by the fire.

[Some spatial databases allow you to have multiple geometry fields, while others are limited to just one per record.]

By itself, a geometry field is simply a database *blob* which can hold the encoded geometry data. The data is usually stored in **Well-Known Binary (WKB)** format. This allows you to store and retrieve geometry data from the database. However, by itself, this isn't very useful—what defines a spatial database is the ability to build a **spatial index** using the stored geometry values.

A spatial index is what allows you to search for records in the database based on their position on the Earth's surface. A spatial index does not index the geometry directly. Instead, it calculates the **bounding box** for each geometry, and then indexes that bounding box. The following illustration shows how this works:

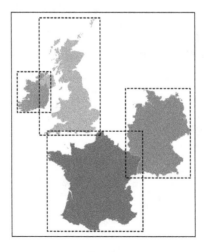

A common task for spatial indexes is to identify the geometry (or geometries) that contain a given point. For example, if the user clicks on a location on a map, you might want to know which country, if any, the user clicked on. This is represented by a spatial database query such as the following:

```
SELECT * FROM table WHERE ST_Contains(table.geometry, click_point);
```

 The `ST_Contains` function is an example of a database query function. This function is provided by the PostGIS spatial database. Different spatial databases use different names for their various query functions; all the query functions listed in this chapter come from PostGIS, as that is the database we'll be working with in this book.

To perform this query, the database first uses the spatial index to identify those records that have a bounding box containing the desired point. This process is shown in the following diagram:

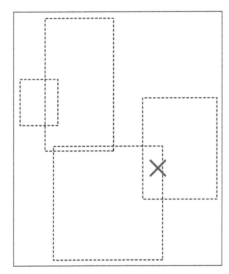

The crosshairs represent the desired point, and the rectangles represent the bounding boxes. As you can see, there are two bounding boxes which contain the desired point. These bounding boxes correspond to the records labeled France and Germany in the database. The database uses this information to load each of the matching geometries into memory and checks each one in turn to see if it contains the desired point:

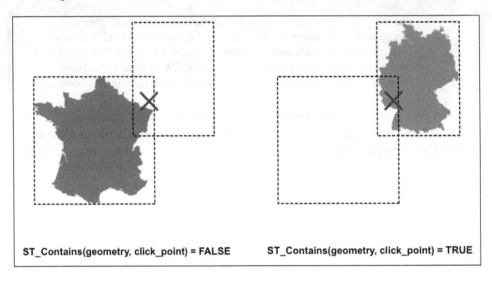

In this way, the database was able to determine that the click point was inside Germany.

Let's review this process, as it is a very important concept. The database *first* identifies the potentially matching records using the bounding boxes stored in the spatial index and *then* loads each potential geometry into memory to check it. This two-step process is surprisingly efficient: by using the bounding boxes in the spatial index, it immediately discards the vast majority of records which are not a potential match. It then performs the relatively time-consuming task of loading the geometry into memory only for the few potential matches, and then checks each of these in turn.

It is important that you understand this two-step process of performing spatial queries because you have to do certain things to make sure it works. In particular:

- You have to ensure that the geometries you want to query against are included in a spatial index.

- You have to carefully phrase your query so that the database can actually use the index you have set up. If, for example, the database has to transform your geometry from one spatial reference system to another, or perform some sort of spatial manipulation on the data before it can be queried against, then your spatial index will be ignored and the database will revert to performing a sequential scan of all your data. This can be extremely slow, taking hours or even days to complete a single query.

- If you have an extremely complex geometry with a large bounding box, for example, a detailed outline of the United States, you may find that your queries are still taking a long time to complete. This is because the bounding box covers such a large area of the Earth's surface that it is being included in many queries, and the complexity of the outline means that the query is still taking a long time to process. One way to solve this problem is to split a large and complex geometry into smaller pieces, so the database only has to process one small piece rather than the whole thing.

Despite these potential issues, a spatial database is a wonderful tool for storing and analyzing geospatial data. Of course, spatial databases are not limited to just searching for records using ST_Contains(). They can be used for all sorts of spatial queries as seen in the following table:

Spatial query function	Description
ST_Within	This matches the records that have a geometry completely enclosed by a given polygon.
ST_Intersects	This matches the records where the record's geometry intersects with a given geometry.
ST_Crosses	This matches the records where the record's geometry crosses over a given line or polygon.
ST_DWithin	This matches the records that are within a given distance of a given location or geometry.

There are some subtleties in these spatial query functions which you will need to become familiar with—these are described in detail in the PostGIS documentation. However, this table should give you an idea of the power of a spatial database and tell you how a spatial database (using the appropriate spatial indexes) can be a great tool for working with geospatial data, especially when you have many records to process.

Now that you have some idea of how a spatial database works, let's install one on your computer and then see how we can access it from within your Python programs.

Installing a spatial database

In this book, we are going to use one of the most popular and powerful geospatial databases: PostGIS. PostGIS is an extension to the freely available PostgreSQL relational database. To use it in our Python programs, we need to install three separate pieces of software:

- The PostgreSQL database server itself
- The PostGIS extension to PostgreSQL
- The psycopg2 database adapter for Python

 PostgreSQL is often referred to simply as **Postgres**. We will use this more colloquial name regularly throughout this book.

Let's work through the process of installing each of these pieces of software in turn.

Installing PostgreSQL

PostgreSQL (http://postgresql.org) is one of the most powerful open source relational databases available. While it has a reputation for being difficult to set up and use, it's not too tricky, and with prebuilt installers available for every major operating system the setup process is now quite straightforward.

Let's go ahead and get PostgreSQL installed on your computer. How you do this depends on which operating system you are running:

- If your computer runs Microsoft Windows, you can download an installer for PostgreSQL from http://www.enterprisedb.com/products-services-training/pgdownload. Select the appropriate installer for your version of Windows (32-bit or 64-bit), and download the installer file. Then simply double-click on the downloaded installer and follow the instructions.

- If you are running Mac OS X, you can download a working version of PostgreSQL from the KyngChaos web site, http://www.kyngchaos.com/software/postgres. Simply download the disk image, open it, and double-click on the **PostgreSQL.pkg** package file to install PostgreSQL on your computer.

- If you are using a Linux machine, you can follow the instructions on the PostgreSQL download page, http://www.postgresql.org/download. Choose the appropriate link for the Linux distribution you are using, and you will be presented with the appropriate installation instructions.

Once you have installed PostgreSQL, you can check that it is running by typing the `psql` command into a terminal or command-line window. If all going well, you should see the Postgres command line:

```
psql (9.3.4)
Type "help" for help.

postgres=#
```

> If the `psql` command complains about user authentication, you may need to specify a user account to use when connecting to Postgres. For example:
>
> `% psql -U postgres`
>
> Many Postgres installations have a `postgres` user, which you need to select (using the `-U` command-line option) when accessing the database. Alternatively, you may need to use `sudo` to switch to the root user, or open the command prompt as an administrator if you are running Microsoft Windows.

Installing PostGIS

Now that we've installed Postgres itself, we next need to install the PostGIS spatial database extension. The main website for PostGIS can be found at `http://postgis.net`. You should go to this website, click on the **Documentation** tab, and download the user manual for the latest version of PostGIS. You'll find this manual very helpful, as it explains PostGIS in great detail, including all the various sorts of queries you can make.

How you install PostGIS depends on which operating system you are running:

- If your computer is running MS Windows, you can download an installer for PostGIS from `http://download.osgeo.org/postgis/windows`.

- For Mac OS X, download and run the PostGIS installer from `http://kyngchaos.com/software/postgres`.

> Note that you will also need to have installed the GDAL Complete package, which you should have already done when working through the previous chapter.

- If you are using a Linux-based operating system, follow the instructions on the PostGIS installation page: `http://postgis.net/install`.

To check that PostGIS has been successfully installed, try typing the following sequence of commands into your terminal window:

```
% createdb test_database
% psql -d test_database -c "CREATE EXTENSION postgis;"
% dropdb test_database
```

 You'll need to add a -U postgres option or use sudo for each of these commands if you need to run PostgreSQL under a different user account.

As you can probably guess, the createdb command creates a new database. We then use the psql command to initialize that database with the PostGIS extension, and finally the dropdb command deletes the database again. If this sequence of commands runs without error, your PostGIS installation (and Postgres itself) is set up and running properly.

Installing psycopg2

Now that we've got a spatial database, let's install the psycopg2 library so we can access it using Python.

psycopg2 is a standard Python database adapter — that is, it's a library that conforms to the Python Database API specified in PEP 249 (https://www.python.org/dev/peps/pep-0249). We will look at how to use psycopg2 to store and query against spatial data, but if you have not worked with a Python database adapter before, you may want to look at one of the available tutorials on the subject. A good tutorial on the subject can be found at http://halfcooked.com/presentations/osdc2006/python_databases.html.

The website for psqcopg2 can be found at http://initd.org/psycopg. As usual, how you install this library depends on which operating system you are using:

- For MS Windows, you can download a double-clickable installer from http://www.stickpeople.com/projects/python/win-psycopg.

- If your computer runs Mac OS X, a double-clickable installer can be found at http://www.kyngchaos.com/software/python.

- For a Linux machine, you will need to install psycopg2 from source. For instructions on how to do this, please refer to http://initd.org/psycopg/docs/install.html.

To check that it worked, start up your Python interpreter and type the following:

```
>>> import psycopg2
>>>
```

If `psycopg2` was installed correctly, you should see the Python interpreter prompt reappear with no error message, as shown in this example. If an error message does appear, you may need to follow the troubleshooting instructions on the `psycopg2` website.

Accessing PostGIS from Python

So far, we have installed some tools and libraries onto your computer. Now it's time to use those tools and libraries to do something interesting. In the remainder of this chapter, we are going to import the World Borders Dataset into a PostGIS database, which we will call `world_borders`, and then use Python to perform various queries against that data. We will also see how we can manipulate that dataset using PostGIS and Python.

To start with, create a new directory named `world_borders` and place it somewhere convenient. You will use this directory to store the various files you create.

Setting up a spatial database

When accessing a database using `psycopg2`, we first have to specify which database we are going to use. This means that the database must exist before your Python code can use it. To set everything up, we'll use the Postgres command-line utilities. Type the following into your terminal or command-line window:

```
% createdb world_borders
```

> Don't forget to include the `-U postgres` option, or `sudo`, if you need to access Postgres under a different user account.

This creates the database itself. We next want to enable the PostGIS spatial extension for our database. To do this, enter the following command:

```
% psql -d world_borders -c "CREATE EXTENSION postgis;"
```

Now that we've set up the database itself, let's create the table within the database which will hold our spatial data. To do this, we're going to create a Python program called `create_table.py`. Go ahead and create this file within your `world_borders` directory, and enter the following into the file:

```
import psycopg2
```

We now want to open up a connection to the database. To do this, we have to tell `psycopg2` which database to use and which user account (and possibly, which password) to use to access that database. This is done by providing keyword parameters to the `psycopg2.connect()` function, like this:

```
connection = psycopg2.connect(database="world_borders",
user="...", password="...")
```

> You'll only need the `user` parameter if you needed to supply a `-U` command-line argument when running the Postgres command-line tools. You'll also only need the `password` if that user account is password-protected.

Once we have a database connection, we then set up a `cursor` object, which we'll use to issue commands to the database:

```
cursor = connection.cursor()
```

The next step may be a bit counter-intuitive: rather than creating the database table, we're going to delete it if it already exists. Doing this lets us run the `create_table.py` script multiple times without causing any errors. Here is the relevant code:

```
cursor.execute("DROP TABLE IF EXISTS borders")
```

The `execute()` statement tells the cursor to run the given SQL command. In this case, the command is `DROP TABLE IF EXISTS`, which tells the database to delete (drop) the table if it already exists.

We can now create our database table using the following command:

```
cursor.execute("CREATE TABLE borders (" +
               "id SERIAL PRIMARY KEY," +
               "name VARCHAR NOT NULL," +
               "iso_code VARCHAR NOT NULL," +
               "outline GEOGRAPHY)")
```

Notice that we have split this command across multiple lines to make it easier to read. With the exception of the last line, this is a standard SQL database table definition: we're creating a table where each record has a unique `id` value automatically allocated by the database, a `name` value, and an `iso_code` value. In the final line, we create the `outline` field and give it a type of GEOGRAPHY. Geography fields are specific to PostGIS; they are a variant of the GEOMETRY field type and are designed to work with spatial data that uses unprojected latitude and longitude coordinates.

Now that we've created our database table, let's set up a spatial index on this data. As we have seen, a spatial index will greatly speed up queries against our database. Let's create a spatial index for our `outline` field:

```
cursor.execute("CREATE INDEX border_index ON borders USING
GIST(outline)")
```

Finally, because Postgres is a transactional database, we need to *commit* the changes we have made, to make them permanent. Here is the necessary code to do this:

```
connection.commit()
```

This finishes our `create_table.py` program, which should look like the following:

```
import psycopg2

connection = psycopg2.connect(database="world_borders",
user="...", password="...")
cursor = connection.cursor()

cursor.execute("DROP TABLE IF EXISTS borders")

cursor.execute("CREATE TABLE borders (" +
               "id SERIAL PRIMARY KEY," +
               "name VARCHAR NOT NULL," +
               "iso_code VARCHAR NOT NULL," +
               "outline GEOGRAPHY)")

cursor.execute("CREATE INDEX border_index ON borders USING
GIST(outline)")
connection.commit()
```

If you run this program, your database table and the associated spatial index will be created. Let's now import the contents of the World Borders Dataset into our newly created table.

Importing spatial data

Take a copy of the TM_WORLD_BORDERS-0.3 directory you downloaded earlier, and place it inside your world_borders directory. Then create another Python script named import_data.py. This is where you will place the code to import the data into your database.

We are going to use the OGR library to import the data from the shapefile, and psycopg2 to insert it into the database. So the first two lines in our program should look like the following:

```
import osgeo.ogr
import psycopg2
```

We next need to open up a connection to the database. The code to do this is identical to the code that we used in the create_table.py script:

```
connection = psycopg2.connect(database="world_borders",
user="...", password="...")
cursor = connection.cursor()
```

 Don't forget to adjust the keyword parameters to psycopg2.connect() to match the user account you need to connect to PostgreSQL.

We are now ready to start importing the data from the shapefile. First, though, we are going to delete the existing contents of our database table; this will let us run our import_data.py program multiple times, wiping out the existing records before adding new ones, so that we start each time with a blank slate:

```
cursor.execute("DELETE FROM borders")
```

We are now ready to import the data from the shapefile into the database. Let's start this by opening the shapefile and extracting the information we want from it, one feature at a time:

```
shapefile = osgeo.ogr.Open("TM_WORLD_BORDERS-0.3/TM_WORLD_BORDERS-
0.3.shp")
layer = shapefile.GetLayer(0)

for i in range(layer.GetFeatureCount()):
    feature  = layer.GetFeature(i)
    name     = feature.GetField("NAME")
    iso_code = feature.GetField("ISO3")
    geometry = feature.GetGeometryRef()
```

This should be familiar to you, since we worked with OGR to read the contents of a shapefile in the previous chapter. Now that we have the geometry, we can convert it into WKT format, like this:

```
wkt = geometry.ExportToWkt()
```

We now have all the information we need to insert the feature into the database. Here is the code to perform the actual insertion:

```
cursor.execute("INSERT INTO borders (name, iso_code, outline)
VALUES (%s, %s, ST_GeogFromText(%s))", (name, iso_code, wkt))
```

There is a lot going on here, so let's take a closer look at this command. We are using INSERT here, which is a standard SQL command. The INSERT command has the following basic structure:

```
INSERT INTO table (field, field, ...) VALUES (value, value, ...);
```

As you can see, we specify the name of the database table, a list of fields, and the values to store into those fields.

As a standard Python database adapter, psycopg2 will automatically translate Python values, such as integers, floating point numbers, strings, datetime objects and the like, into their SQL equivalents. This is where those %s placeholders come in—we use %s in our SQL command string at each point where we want to provide a value, and then supply the actual values themselves as the second parameter to the cursor.execute() command. Consider, for example, the following Postgres command:

```
cursor.execute("INSERT INTO users (name, age) VALUES (%s, %s)",
(user_name, user_age))
```

This command would insert a record into the users table, setting the name field to the value of the user_name variable, and the age field to the value of the user_age variable. This conversion of Python values to SQL string literals is extremely powerful and is one of the major benefits of using a database adapter.

There is one final complexity in the INSERT statement we are using to import the shapefile's contents into our borders table: we are using the ST_GeogFromText() function to convert our WKT-format string into a geography value before inserting it into the outline field. We have to do this because OGR and Postgres use different internal representations for geometry data. WKT format strings are the *lingua franca* that converts between these two internal representations.

After we have finished importing the various features from the shapefile, we have to commit our changes so that they are written to the database:

```
connection.commit()
```

Putting all of this together, here's what our `import_data.py` program looks like:

```
import osgeo.ogr
import psycopg2

connection = psycopg2.connect(database="world_borders",
user="...", password="...")
cursor = connection.cursor()

cursor.execute("DELETE FROM borders")

shapefile = osgeo.ogr.Open("TM_WORLD_BORDERS-0.3.shp")
layer = shapefile.GetLayer(0)

for i in range(layer.GetFeatureCount()):
    feature = layer.GetFeature(i)
    name = feature.GetField("NAME")
    iso_code = feature.GetField("ISO3")
    geometry = feature.GetGeometryRef()
    wkt = geometry.ExportToWkt()

    cursor.execute("INSERT INTO borders (name, iso_code, outline)
VALUES (%s, %s, ST_GeogFromText(%s))", (name, iso_code, wkt))

connection.commit()
```

When we run this program, all the records from the World Borders Dataset shapefile should be imported into the database. Notice that it only takes a few seconds to complete—even though we have to convert the outlines from OGR geometries into WKT, and then convert from WKT into PostGIS geography objects, it does not take long to do this.

If you want, you can run the `psql` command-line client and type commands such as `SELECT id,name,iso_code FROM borders` to see the data that you have imported. But of course we really want to use Python to query against our spatial database. Let's do this now.

Querying spatial data

Let's write another Python program to perform various queries against the contents of our database. Start by creating another Python file named `query_data.py` and place it into the `world_borders` directory. We start by importing the `psycopg2` library, opening up a connection to our database, and creating a database cursor:

```
import psycopg2
connection = psycopg2.connect(database="world_borders", user="...",
password="...")
cursor = connection.cursor()
```

This should all be familiar from the `create_table.py` program we created earlier.

Let's now perform a simple (non-spatial) database query, just to see how it works. Add the following to the end of your program:

```
cursor.execute("SELECT id,name FROM borders ORDER BY name")
for row in cursor:
    print row
```

When you run your `query_data.py` program, you should see a list of the record IDs and associated names, taken from your `borders` table:

```
(1264, 'Afghanistan')
(1237, 'Albania')
(1235, 'Algeria')
...
```

Notice that you use `cursor.execute()` to execute your query, and then iterate over the cursor to get the matching rows. The value for each row is a tuple containing the fields you requested.

> Of course, you can also use `%s` to include Python values in your query, for example:
> ```
> cursor.execute("SELECT id FROM borders WHERE name=%s",
> (country_name,))
> ```

So far, we have been using the non-spatial aspects of PostgreSQL. Let's now make a spatial query against this data. We're going to ask the database to identify all countries within 1,000 kilometers of Paris. Using the `GEOGRAPHY` data type in PostGIS, this is easy to do:

```
lat   = 48.8567
long  = 2.3508
```

```
    radius = 1000000

    cursor.execute("SELECT name FROM borders WHERE ST_DWITHIN(" +
                   "ST_MakePoint(%s, %s), outline, %s)", (long,
    lat, radius))
    for row in cursor:
        print row[0]
```

The ST_DWithin command identifies the countries that are within radius meters of the specified point; running the program should return a list of the countries that are within 1,000 kilometers of Paris:

```
San Marino
Denmark
Ireland
Austria
...
Switzerland
United Kingdom
```

This gives you an idea of how powerful PostGIS is, and the types of queries you can make using the psycopg2 database adapter. Make sure you study the *PostGIS Reference* section of the PostGIS manual to learn about the various sorts of spatial queries you can make.

Manipulating spatial data

You are not limited to just using static data in your spatial analysis. You can also create new geometries and manipulate existing geometries directly within a PostGIS database. While it's easy to create a brand new geometry using functions such as the ST_GeogFromText() function we used earlier, you can also use the PostGIS geometry editing and geometry processing functions to create new geography values derived from old ones.

 There are some limitations on the functions available when you use the PostGIS GEOGRAPHY type. PostGIS originally only supported the GEOMETRY data type, which was designed to only work with spatial data projected onto a flat Cartesian plane. When using the GEOGRAPHY field, check the PostGIS manual to see which functions are supported.

To get an idea of how we can calculate new spatial values based on our existing data, let's write a program to buffer our outlines, and store them into a new GEOGRAPHY column in our database table.

We saw the `buffer()` operation in the previous chapter, where we saw that it can often be used to fix an invalid geometry. If you remember, the `buffer()` operation constructs a new geometry that includes all points within a certain distance of the existing geometry. The following image shows the outline of the United Kingdom, and the same outline after it has been buffered:

Let's write a program to calculate these buffered outlines. Create a new Python script in your `world_borders` directory, and name it `buffer.py`. Enter the following into this file:

```
import psycopg2
connection = psycopg2.connect(database="world_borders", user="...",
password="...")
cursor = connection.cursor()
```

We now want to create a new field to hold the buffered outline. To do this, add the following to the end of your file:

```
try:
    cursor.execute("ALTER TABLE borders ADD COLUMN
buffered_outline GEOGRAPHY")
except psycopg2.ProgrammingError:
    connection.rollback()
```

The ALTER TABLE command is a standard Postgres command to change the structure of a database table; in this case, we add a new GEOGRAPHY column named buffered_outline.

Notice that we wrapped our ALTER TABLE command in a try...except statement. This is because psycopg2 will raise ProgrammingError if the column already exists. By catching this error, we can run our buffer.py program multiple times without it failing because the buffered_outline field has already been added to the table.

Because of transaction issues with exceptions in psycopg2, we have to call connection.rollback() when an exception occurs. This allows the program to continue even though an exception has been raised.

Our next task is to calculate the buffered outlines. Using PostGIS, this is very easy:

```
cursor.execute("UPDATE borders SET
buffered_outline=ST_Buffer(outline, 1000)")
```

In this SQL statement, we are setting the value of the buffered_outline field to the result of the ST_Buffer() command. The ST_Buffer() command accepts a geography value and a distance in meters; it returns a new geography that contains all points that are within the given distance from the existing geography.

Our final task is to commit the changes we have made to the database:

```
connection.commit()
```

This actually completes our buffer.py program, and if we run it, we will get a buffered version of each outline stored in the buffered_outline field. However, because this program does not show anything, there's no way of knowing if it actually worked. To get around this, let's add a final spatial query to calculate and display the area of each outline.

The basic structure of our query will look like the following:

```
cursor.execute("SELECT name, ST_Area(outline), ST_Area(buffered_
outline) FROM borders ORDER BY name")
for name, area1, area2 in cursor:
    ...
```

The result of the ST_Area() function is the area of the geography measured in square meters. Because these numbers can be huge, we'll want to convert them into square kilometers for display. However, there is a slight problem: when we buffer a geometry, it can sometimes become invalid because the buffered geometry lies outside the range of valid latitude and longitude values. Even though we only buffered the geographies by a kilometer, any geographies that lie close to the north or south pole, or close to the limits of -180 or +180 degrees of longitude, will have an invalid buffered outline. When we try to calculate the area of these invalid outlines, the result will be a NaN (Not a Number) value.

Let's add some code to check for invalid areas and handle them gracefully; replace the . . . line in the previous code listing with the following:

```
if not math.isnan(area1):
    area1 = int(area1/1000000)
else:
    area1 = "n/a"
if not math.isnan(area2):
    area2 = int(area2/1000000)
else:
    area2 = "n/a"
print name, area1, area2
```

You will also need to add an import math statement to the top of your program.

Running this program will take a minute or so to calculate all the buffers, after which the calculated areas will be displayed:

```
Afghanistan 641915 646985
Albania 28676 29647
Algeria 2317478 2324740
American Samoa 229 363
...
Zimbabwe 389856 392705
Åland Islands 817 1144
```

As you can see, the buffered area is somewhat larger than the original one, which is what you would expect.

Exporting spatial data

Our introduction to spatial databases is almost complete; the only thing left to examine is how to get spatial data out of PostGIS again, for example to save it back into a shapefile. To extract a spatial value from a GEOGRAPHY field, use the ST_AsText() function. For example:

```
cursor.execute("SELECT name,ST_AsText(outline) FROM borders")
for name,wkt in cursor:
    geometry = osgeo.ogr.CreateGeometryFromWkt(wkt)
    ...
```

You can then use the OGR geometry to write the spatial data into a shapefile, or do anything else you wish to do with it.

Summary

In this chapter, we looked at how spatial databases can be a powerful tool for geospatial data analysis. We covered the important concepts behind spatial databases, and installed PostgreSQL, PostGIS, and psycopg2 onto your computer. We then got our hands dirty by creating a spatial database, importing data into that database, performing spatial queries, manipulating spatial data using PostGIS, and exporting data from a spatial database, all using Python code.

In the next chapter, we will explore how to use the Mapnik library to produce great-looking maps based on our geospatial data.

4
Creating Maps

In this chapter, we will look at how Python programs can create great-looking maps using the Mapnik library. You will install Mapnik onto your computer, learn the basics of the Mapnik library, and see how you can use it to generate simple maps. We will then explore some of the more advanced aspects of Mapnik, and see how it can be used to produce a wide range of complex visual effects. Finally, we will create a useful program that displays the contents of any shapefile as a map.

Introducing Mapnik

It is very difficult to make sense of geospatial data without being able to visualize it. The usual way in which spatial data is made visible is by drawing a map—indeed, a map is nothing more than an image created out of spatial data. **Mapnik** (http://mapnik.org) is a powerful tool for transforming raw geospatial data into a map image.

Mapnik itself is written in C++ but comes with bindings that allow you to access it from Python. Using Python code, you can define the various layers that make up a map, specify the datasources containing the data to be displayed, and then set up the styles which control how the various features are to be drawn.

Mapnik can be a little intimidating when you first start working with it, so let's jump in and get our hands dirty right away. Let's start by installing Mapnik onto your computer and use it to generate a simple map, before delving a bit deeper into how to build and style maps using the Mapnik library.

Installing Mapnik

To install Mapnik, go to the downloads page on the main Mapnik website (`http://mapnik.org/download`), and choose the installer for your operating system. Pre-built packages are available for both Mac OS X and MS Windows. For Linux machines, you will need to either compile the program from source, or use a package manager to download, compile, and install Mapnik and its various dependencies; full instructions on how to do this are provided on the Mapnik download page.

A taste of Mapnik

We will start our exploration of Mapnik by writing a simple program that generates a map using the World Borders Dataset we downloaded earlier. Copy the contents of the `TM_WORLD_BORDERS-0.3` directory into a convenient place, and then create a new Python program in the same directory. Name your new program `mapnik_example.py`. This program will generate a PNG-format image file based on the contents of the World Borders Dataset shapefile.

Type the following into your `mapnik_example.py` file:

```python
import mapnik

map = mapnik.Map(1200, 600)
map.background = mapnik.Color("#e0e0ff")

layer = mapnik.Layer("countries")
layer.datasource = mapnik.Shapefile(file="TM_WORLD_BORDERS-
0.3.shp")
layer.styles.append("country_style")
map.layers.append(layer)

fill_symbol = mapnik.PolygonSymbolizer(mapnik.Color("#60a060"))
line_symbol = mapnik.LineSymbolizer(mapnik.Color("black"), 0.5)

rule = mapnik.Rule()
rule.symbols.append(fill_symbol)
rule.symbols.append(line_symbol)

style = mapnik.Style()
style.rules.append(rule)

map.append_style("country_style", style)

map.zoom_all()
mapnik.render_to_file(map, "map.png", "png")
```

When you run this program, a new file named `map.png` should be created in the same directory. Opening this file will display the generated map:

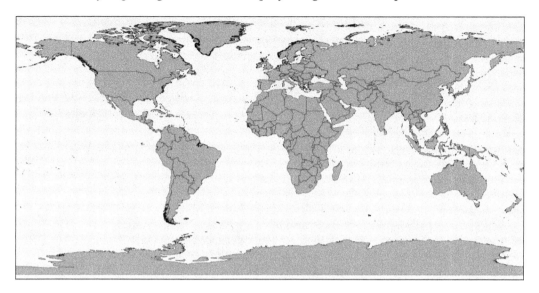

Now that we've seen what our example program does, let's take a closer look at it and examine each part in turn. Let's start with the very beginning of our program:

```
import mapnik

map = mapnik.Map(1200, 600)
map.background = mapnik.Color("#e0e0ff")
```

Here we simply import the Mapnik library, and then create and initialize a new **map** object. The map image will be 1,200 pixels wide and 600 pixels high, and the map will have a pale blue background defined by the hexadecimal color value `#e0e0ff`.

A map consists of one or more **map layers**. In our program, we only have one map layer, which we set up to access the TM_WORLD_BORDERS shapefile:

```
layer = mapnik.Layer("countries")
layer.datasource = mapnik.Shapefile(file="TM_WORLD_BORDERS-0.3.shp")
layer.styles.append("country_style")
map.layers.append(layer)
```

There are a few things to notice about this layer definition:

- Each map layer is given a **name** which uniquely identifies the layer within the map; in our program, we've called our map layer `countries`.

- Each layer has a **datasource** which tells Mapnik where the data should come from. In this case, we're using the `mapnik.Shapefile` class to load the data from a shapefile, though there are many different types of datasources that can be used. For example, you can load data directly from a spatial database, or even use a Python datasource to create and display features programmatically.

- The `layer.styles.append("country_style")` line tells Mapnik which **style** to use to draw the layer's data. Mapnik styles are referred to by name, and you can have any number of styles associated with each layer.

> Mapnik layers can also have a spatial reference system associated with them. If you don't specify a spatial reference system, Mapnik will assume that the data is in the standard EPSG 4326 spatial reference system.

We next want to define the `country_style` style which will draw the contents of our map layer. A style consists of any number of **rules**, where each rule has an optional **filter** identifying which of the features in the datasource should be drawn using this rule, and a list of **symbolizers** which will be used to draw the matching features onto the map.

We start by creating two symbolizers: one to fill the interior of each polygon with a faded green color, and another to draw the outline of each polygon using a thin black line:

```
fill_symbol = mapnik.PolygonSymbolizer(mapnik.Color("#60a060"))
line_symbol = mapnik.LineSymbolizer(mapnik.Color("black"), 0.5)
```

For the fill symbol, we are once again using a hexadecimal color code to define the color to use to draw the interior of the polygon, while for the line symbol we make use of a named color. Note that the `0.5` value defines the width, in pixels, to use to draw the outline of each polygon.

Now that we have our two symbolizers, we next define a rule which uses them to draw the contents of the shapefile:

```
rule = mapnik.Rule()
rule.symbols.append(fill_symbol)
rule.symbols.append(line_symbol)
```

Notice that this rule has no filter; the absence of a filter tells Mapnik that every feature in the layer's datasource should be drawn using these two symbolizers.

To finish defining our `country_style` style, we initialize the `Style` object itself, add our one-and-only rule to the style, and then add the style object to our map:

```
style = mapnik.Style()
style.rules.append(rule)

map.append_style("country_style", style)
```

Notice that we give the style a name when we add it to the map object; because this name is used to identify the styles used by the map layer, it is important that we use exactly the same name both when adding the style to the map and when referring to the style in the map layer.

Our final task is to tell the map which area of the world to display, and how to **render** the visible portion of the map into an image file:

```
map.zoom_all()
mapnik.render_to_file(map, "map.png", "png")
```

In our example, we are zooming out to show all the data in the map layer, and saving the results to a PNG format image file named `map.png`.

This completes our example Python program to generate a map image using Mapnik. There are lots of more sophisticated things you can do using Mapnik, but this will give you an idea of how it works and what you can do with it.

Building a map

Now that we've seen an example of how Mapnik works, let's look more closely at some of the ideas behind the Mapnik library. Consider, for example, the following map of the west coast of the United States:

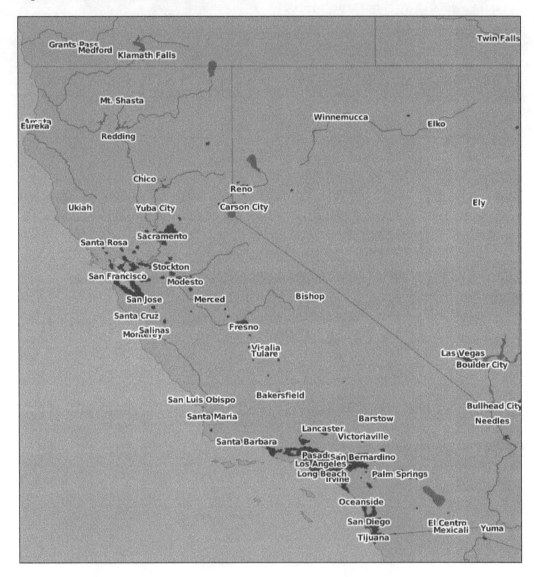

This map is actually made up of four different map layers:

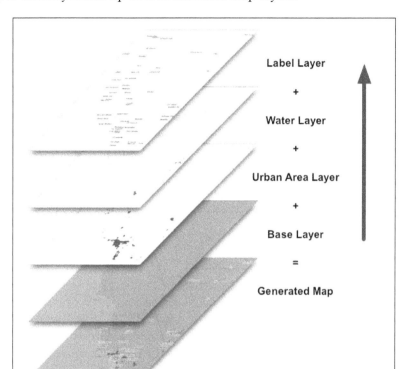

As you can see, the map layers are drawn one on top of the other, as indicated by the arrow on the right-hand side of the diagram. In order to achieve the right visual effect, the layers need to be added in *reverse* order, so that each layer added will appear in front of the layers already in the map. That is, the base layer should be added first, then the urban area layer, and so on. The order in which the layers are added to the map is very important; if you get the order wrong, some of your layers will be obscured.

Styling a map

As we saw earlier, the map's styles are defined by creating mapnik.Style objects and adding them to the map, giving each one a unique name:

```
style = mapnik.Style()
# ...setup style
map.append_style("style_name", style)
```

We then tell each map layer which styles we want that layer to use by adding the style name to the layer's `styles` list:

```
layer.styles.append("style_name")
```

You might think that it would be easier to simply add the style definition directly to the map layer, but this process of referring to styles by name is deliberate: it separates *what* will be displayed from *how* it is displayed. This approach lets you use the same set of styles across multiple map layers, or completely alter the appearance of your map just by swapping style names.

> There is an alternative way of defining your map styles. Rather than creating your own `mapnik.Style` objects and adding them to the map one at a time, you can define all your styles at once using an XML-format stylesheet. While this is very powerful, XML stylesheets are rather hard to read and very un-Pythonic. For these reasons, we won't be using XML stylesheets in this book.

In our example program, we created a single `mapnik.Style` object that consisted of just one rule. This rule had two symbolizers associated with it, telling Mapnik how to draw the interior and exterior of each country's polygon. Rules can be more sophisticated, however, including various *conditions* which must be met before the rule is used. For example, consider the following Python code snippet:

```
symbol1 = ...
symbol2 = ...
symbol3 = ...

rule1 = mapnik.Rule()
rule1.filter = mapnik.Filter("[POPULATION] < 500000")
rule1.symbols.append(symbol1)

rule2 = mapnik.Rule()
rule.filter = mapnik.Filter("[POPULATION] < 1000000")
rule2.symbols.append(symbol2)

rule3 = mapnik.Rule()
rule3.set_else(True)
rule3.symbols.append(symbol3)

style.rules.append(rule1)
style.rules.append(rule2)
style.rules.append(rule3)
```

Because the style's rules are evaluated one after the other, this style will draw the feature using symbol1 if the feature's POPULATION attribute has a value of less than 500,000; it will draw the feature using symbol2 if the feature's POPULATION attribute has a value between 500,000 and 1,000,000; and it will draw the feature using symbol3 if the feature's POPULATION attribute is 1,000,000 or more.

As well as having filters, rules can also have a minimum and maximum scale factor at which the rule will apply. This can be used, for example, to hide smaller features when the map is zoomed right out.

Because you can have multiple symbols within a rule, the way that features are drawn can also get quite sophisticated. For example, you could define a single rule which uses three separate symbolizers to draw a LineString geometry as a street:

As you can imagine, combining symbolizers, rules, filters, and styles will give you tremendous flexibility in choosing which features should appear within a map, and how those features will be drawn.

Learning Mapnik

Now that you've seen what Mapnik can do and have some idea of how Mapnik works, let's look more deeply at some of the other aspects of the Mapnik library. We will be covering datasources, symbolizers, and map rendering in this section of the chapter.

Datasources

Each map layer is associated with a **datasource** (a subclass of mapnik.Datasource) that provides the data to be displayed on the map. The various types of datasources are made available through C++ plugins, which are enabled or disabled when Mapnik is compiled. To see if a given type of datasource is available, you check to see if the associated plugin has been installed into your copy of Mapnik. You can see a list of the installed plugins (and therefore, the supported datasources) by typing the following into the Python command prompt:

```
import mapnik
print list(mapnik.DatasourceCache.plugin_names())
```

The following datasource plugins are currently supported by Mapnik:

- **csv**: This plugin provides the `mapnik.CSV` datasource, which reads tabular data from either a text file or a string. By default, the data is in **CSV (comma-separated value)** format, though other similar formats are also supported.

  The CSV datasource will automatically identify point geometries based on columns with headers containing names like "lat", "latitude", "lon", "long", and "longitude". The datasource will also detect GeoJSON and WKT formatted geometries if the column header is named "geojson" or "wkt". Documentation for the `csv` plugin can be found at `https://github.com/mapnik/mapnik/wiki/CSV-Plugin`.

- **gdal**: This plugin provides the `mapnik.Gdal` datasource. This datasource uses the GDAL library to read raster-format data and make it available to the map layer. To use this datasource in a map layer, you need to add a style to the map layer which includes a `mapnik.RasterSymbolizer` to draw the raster data onto the map. Documentation for the `gdal` plugin can be found at `https://github.com/mapnik/mapnik/wiki/GDAL`.

- **ogr**: This plugin implements the `mapnik.Ogr` datasource. This datasource uses the OGR library to read vector-format data. Documentation for the `ogr` plugin can be found at `https://github.com/mapnik/mapnik/wiki/OGR`.

- **osm**: The `osm` plugin provides the `mapnik.Osm` datasource. This datasource reads data in OpenStreetMap XML format. Documentation for the `osm` plugin can be found at `https://github.com/mapnik/mapnik/wiki/OsmPlugin`.

- **postgis**: This plugin provides the `mapnik.PostGIS` datasource. This datasource connects to a PostGIS database and reads spatial data from a specified database table. You use the `host`, `dbname`, `user`, and `password` parameters when creating a PostGIS datasource to tell Mapnik how to connect to a given PostGIS database, while the `table` parameter specifies which table in the database to read the data from.

  Additional parameters are available for special purposes, for example to limit the extent of the data to display, or to use an SQL subquery to include only some of the records in the database table. Complete documentation for the postgis plugin can be found at `https://github.com/mapnik/mapnik/wiki/PostGIS`.

- **python**: This plugin provides the `mapnik.Python` datasource. This allows you to implement your own datasource by writing a custom Python class that provides access to the data to be displayed. To write a custom Python datasource, you would typically create a subclass of `mapnik.PythonDatasource` and then use the name of your custom class as the `factory` parameter when calling the mapnik.Python() function to instantiate your datasource. You then implement the necessary methods within your class to provide access to the data. Documentation for the python plugin can be found at `https://github.com/mapnik/mapnik/wiki/Python-Plugin`.

- **raster**: This plugin implements the `mapnik.Raster` datasource, which displays the contents of a raster image file in either TIFF or GeoTIFF format. While you can also read raster-format data using the `gdal` plugin, the `raster` plugin is faster when reading these types of files. To use this datasource in a map layer, you need to add a style to the map layer which includes a `RasterSymbolizer` to draw the contents of the image file onto the map. Documentation for the `raster` plugin can be found at `https://github.com/mapnik/mapnik/wiki/Raster`.

- **shape**: This plugin provides the `mapnik.Shapefile` datasource, which allows you to read shapefiles. While the `ogr` datasource is also able to read shapefiles, it is often more convenient to use the `mapnik.Shapefile` datasource. Documentation for the `shape` plugin can be found at `https://github.com/mapnik/mapnik/wiki/ShapeFile`.

- **sqlite**: This plugin provides the `mapnik.SQLite` datasource. This datasource reads spatial data from an SQLite database. The database can either be an ordinary SQLite database holding geometry data in WKB format, or a spatially-enabled database using the Spatialite database extension. Documentation for the `sqlite` plugin can be found at `https://github.com/mapnik/mapnik/wiki/SQLite`.

Symbolizers

Symbolizers do the actual work of drawing a feature onto the map. Multiple symbolizers are often used to draw a single feature—we saw this earlier when we used a `PolygonSymbolizer` to draw the interior of a polygon together with a `LineSymbolizer` to draw the polygon's outline.

There are many different types of symbolizers available within Mapnik, and many of the symbolizers have complex options associated with them. Rather than exhaustively listing all the symbolizers and their various options, we will instead just look at some of the more common types of symbolizers and how they can be used.

PointSymbolizer

The PointSymbolizer class is used to draw an image centered over a Point geometry. By default, each point is displayed as a 4 x 4 pixel black square:

To use a different image, you have to create a mapnik.PathExpression object to represent the path to the desired image file, and then pass that to the PointSymbolizer object when you instantiate it:

```
path = mapnik.PathExpression("/path/to/image.png")
point_symbol = PointSymbolizer(path)
```

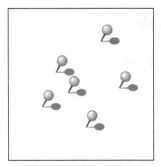

Note that PointSymbolizer draws the image centered on the desired point. To use a drop-pin image as shown in the preceding example, you will need to add extra transparent whitespace so that the tip of the pin is in the middle of the image, like this:

You can control the opacity of the drawn image by setting the symbolizer's `opacity` attribute. You can also control whether labels will be drawn on top of the image by setting the `allow_overlap` attribute to `True`. Finally, you can apply an SVG transformation to the image by setting the `transform` attribute to a string containing a standard SVG transformation expression, for example `point_symbol.transform = "rotate(45)"`.

Documentation for the PointSymbolizer can be found at `https://github.com/mapnik/mapnik/wiki/PointSymbolizer`.

LineSymbolizer

A `mapnik.LineSymbolizer` is used to draw LineString geometries and the outlines of Polygon geometries. When you create a new LineSymbolizer, you would typically configure it using two parameters: the color to use to draw the line as a `mapnik.Color` object, and the width of the line, measured in pixels. For example:

```
line_symbol = mapnik.LineSymbolizer(mapnik.Color("black"), 0.5)
```

Notice that you can use fractional line widths; because Mapnik uses anti-aliasing, a line narrower than 1 pixel will often look better than a line with an integer width if you are drawing many lines close together.

In addition to the color and the width, you can also make the line semi-transparent by setting the `opacity` attribute. This should be set to a number between 0.0 and 1.0, where 0.0 means the line will be completely transparent and 1.0 means the line will be completely opaque.

You can also use the `stroke` attribute to get access to (or replace) the stroke object used by the line symbolizer. The stroke object, an instance of `mapnik.Stroke`, can be used for more complicated visual effects. For example, you can create a dashed line effect by calling the stroke's `add_dash()` method:

```
line_symbol.stroke.add_dash(5, 7)
```

Both numbers are measured in pixels; the first number is the length of the dash segment, while the second is the length of the gap between dashes.

 Note that you can create alternating dash patterns by calling `add_dash()` more than once.

You can also set the stroke's `line_cap` attribute to control how the ends of the line should be drawn, and the stroke's `line_join` attribute to control how the joins between the individual line segments are drawn whenever the LineString changes direction. The `line_cap` attribute can be set to one of the following values:

```
mapnik.line_cap.BUTT_CAP
mapnik.line_cap.ROUND_CAP
mapnik.line_cap.SQUARE_CAP
```

The `line_join` attribute can be set to one of the following:

```
mapnik.line_join.MITER_JOIN
mapnik.line_join.ROUND_JOIN
mapnik.line_join.BEVEL_JOIN
```

Documentation for the `LineSymbolizer` class can be found at `https://github.com/mapnik/mapnik/wiki/LineSymbolizer`.

PolygonSymbolizer

The `mapnik.PolygonSymbolizer` class is used to fill the interior of a Polygon geometry with a given color. When you create a new PolygonSymbolizer, you would typically pass it a single parameter: the `mapnik.Color` object to use to fill the polygon. You can also change the opacity of the symbolizer by setting the `fill_opacity` attribute, for example:

```
fill_symbol.fill_opacity = 0.8
```

Once again, the opacity is measured from 0.0 (completely transparent) to 1.0 (completely opaque).

There is one other PolygonSymbolizer attribute which you might find useful: `gamma`. The `gamma` value can be set to a number between 0.0 and 1.0. The `gamma` value controls the amount of anti-aliasing used to draw the edge of the polygon; with the default `gamma` value of `1.0`, the edges of the polygon will be fully anti-aliased. While this is usually a good thing, if you try to draw adjacent polygons with the same color, the antialiasing will cause the edges of the polygons to be visible rather than combining them into a single larger area. By turning down the gamma slightly (for example, `fill_symbol.gamma = 0.6`), the edges between adjacent polygons will disappear.

Documentation for the `PolygonSymbolizer` class can be found at `https://github.com/mapnik/mapnik/wiki/PolygonSymbolizer`.

TextSymbolizer

The TextSymbolizer class is used to draw textual labels onto a map. This type of symbolizer can be used for point, LineString, and Polygon geometries. The following example shows how a TextSymbolizer can be used:

```
text_symbol = mapnik.TextSymbolizer(mapnik.Expresion("[label]"),
"DejaVu Sans Book", 10, mapnik.Color("black"))
```

As you can see, four parameters are typically passed to the TextSymbolizer's initializer:

- A mapnik.Expression object defining the text to be displayed. In this case, the text to be displayed will come from the label attribute in the datasource.
- The name of the font to use for drawing the text. To see what fonts are available, type the following into the Python command line:

```
import mapnik
for font in mapnik.FontEngine.face_names():
    print font
```

- The font size, measured in pixels.
- The color to use to draw the text.

By default, the text will be drawn in the center of the geometry; for example:

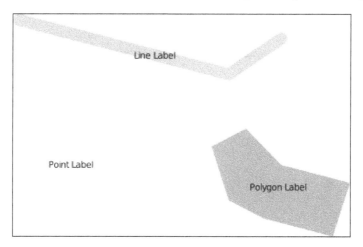

This positioning of the label is called **point placement**. The TextSymbolizer allows you to change this to use what is called **line placement**, where the label will be drawn along the lines:

```
text_symbol.label_placement =
mapnik.label_placement.LINE_PLACEMENT
```

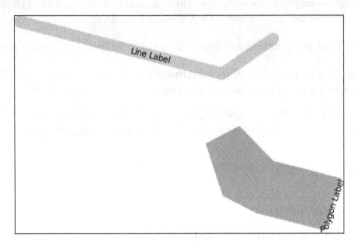

As you can see, this causes the label to be drawn along the length of a LineString geometry, or along the perimeter of a Polygon. The text won't be drawn at all for a Point geometry, since there are no lines within a point.

The TextSymbolizer will normally just draw the label once, but you can tell the symbolizer to repeat the label if you wish by specifying a pixel gap to use between each label:

```
text_symbol.label_spacing = 30
```

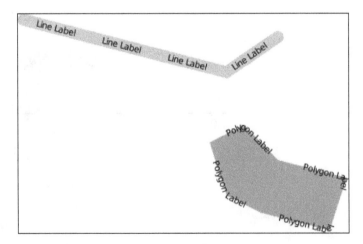

By default, Mapnik is smart enough to stop labels from overlapping each other. If possible, it moves the label slightly to avoid an overlap, and then hides the label completely if it would still overlap. For example:

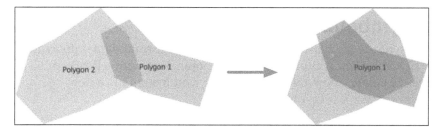

You can change this by setting the `allow_overlap` attribute:

```
text_symbol.allow_overlap = True
```

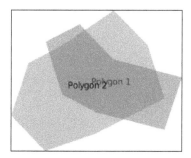

Finally, you can set a halo effect to draw a lighter-colored border around the text so that it is visible even against a dark background. For example,

```
text_symbol.halo_fill = mapnik.Color("white")
text_symbol.halo_radius = 1
```

There are many more labeling options, all of which are described at length in the documentation for the TextSymbolizer class. This can be found at https://github.com/mapnik/mapnik/wiki/TextSymbolizer.

RasterSymbolizer

The RasterSymbolizer class is used to draw raster-format data onto a map. This type of symbolizer is typically used in conjunction with a Raster or GDAL datasource. To create a new raster symbolizer, you instantiate a new mapnik.RasterSymbolizer object:

```
raster_symbol = mapnik.RasterSymbolizer()
```

The raster symbolizer will automatically draw any raster-format data provided by the map layer's datasource. This is often used to draw a basemap onto which the vector data is to be displayed; for example:

While there are some advanced options to control the way the raster data is displayed, in most cases, the only option you might be interested in is the opacity attribute. As usual, this sets the opacity for the displayed image, allowing you to layer semi-transparent raster images one on top of the other.

Documentation for the RasterSymbolizer can be found at https://github.com/mapnik/mapnik/wiki/RasterSymbolizer.

Map rendering

We have now examined in detail many of the building blocks for generating maps: layers, datasources, styles, rules, filters, and symbolizers. Using what you have learned, you should be able to build and style your own maps. But what can you do with a `mapnik.Map` object once you have set one up?

In the example program we examined at the start of this chapter, we used the `mapnik.render_to_file()` function to save the generated map into an image file. When rendering the map, you first have to set the map's **extent**—that is, the rectangle that defines the visible portion of the map:

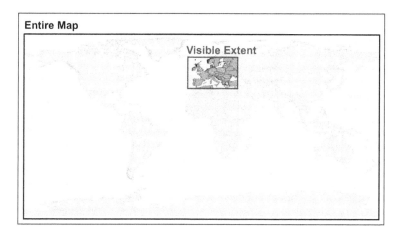

Only the visible extent of the map will be included in the generated image; everything else will be ignored.

In our example program, we used `map.zoom_all()` to set the visible extent of the map to include all the features in all the map layers. Of course, there are times when you only want to display part of the overall map. To do this, you can use the `map.zoomToBox()` method to set the visible extent of the map. For example:

```
map.zoomToBox(mapnik.Box2d(-124.5, 32.0, -114.0, 43.0))
```

The four numbers represent the minimum longitude, the minimum latitude, the maximum longitude, and the maximum latitude, respectively. If you execute this statement using these latitude and longitude values, the visible extent of the map will cover approximately the American state of California.

Note that you aren't limited to only rendering a map once. If you want, you can create multiple images from a single `mapnik.Map` object, changing the visible extent and then calling `mapnik.render_to_file()` to save the newly-visible portion of the map to a different file each time.

A working example

Let's put together everything that we have learned to write a program that can display the contents of a shapefile. This is quite a useful program to have, as you can manipulate or generate some spatial data, save the results into a shapefile, and then run this program to display the shapefile's contents as a generated map image.

We'll call our program `shapeToMap.py`. Create this file, and start entering the following Python code into it:

```python
import mapnik

LAYERS = [
    {'shapefile' : "TM_WORLD_BORDERS-0.3.shp",
     'lineColor' : "black",
     'lineWidth' : 0.4,
     'fillColor' : "#709070",
     'labelField' : "NAME",
     'labelSize' : 12,
     'labelColor' : "black"
    }
]

BACKGROUND_COLOR = "#a0c0ff"

BOUNDS_MIN_LAT  = 35.26
BOUNDS_MAX_LAT  = 71.39
BOUNDS_MIN_LONG = -10.90
BOUNDS_MAX_LONG = 41.13

MAX_WIDTH  = 1600
MAX_HEIGHT = 800
```

Note that the various constants we have defined here will be used to configure the map that we are going to generate:

- LAYERS: This is a list of the map layers to display on the map. Each item in this list should be a dictionary with all or some of following entries:
    - `shapefile`: The name and path of the desired shapefile
    - `lineColor`: The hexadecimal color code to use to draw the feature's exterior, if any
    - `lineWidth`: The width of the line to use to draw the feature's exterior, measured in pixels

- ° `fillColor`: The hexadecimal color code to use to draw the feature's interior, if any

- ° `labelField`: The name of the attribute in the source file to use to label each feature, if any

- ° `labelSize`: The font size to use when labeling the features, measured in pixels

- ° `labelColor`: The hexadecimal color code to use to draw the label

- `BACKGROUND_COLOR`: This is the hexadecimal color code to use to draw the background of the map.

- `BOUNDS_MIN_LAT`, `BOUNDS_MIN_LONG`, `BOUNDS_MAX_LAT`, and `BOUNDS_MAX_LONG`: These define the visible extent of the map you want to generate.

- `MAX_WIDTH` and `MAX_HEIGHT`: These specify the maximum size of the generated map image. Note that the generated image may actually be smaller than these values, depending on the aspect ratio of the bounding rectangle.

Whenever you want to generate a map using this program, you will need to edit these constants to suit your requirements.

We next need to calculate the height and width to use for our map. Because the visible extent can be any shape, we calculate the actual width and height to be as large as possible while matching the aspect ratio of the visible extent. We do this by first calculating the map's width and height so that the width is the maximum allowable width, and the height is whatever is needed to match the aspect ratio of the visible extent. To do this, add the following code to the end of your program:

```
extent = mapnik.Envelope(BOUNDS_MIN_LONG, BOUNDS_MIN_LAT,
BOUNDS_MAX_LONG, BOUNDS_MAX_LAT)
aspectRatio = extent.width() / extent.height()

mapWidth = MAX_WIDTH
mapHeight = int(mapWidth / aspectRatio)
```

We next see if the calculated height is too big, and if so, scale down the map so that the height is no bigger than the allowable maximum:

```
if mapHeight > MAX_HEIGHT:
    scaleFactor = float(MAX_HEIGHT) / float(mapHeight)
    mapWidth = int(mapWidth * scaleFactor)
    mapHeight = int(mapHeight * scaleFactor)
```

This ensures that the generated map is as large as possible, while ensuring the map has the same aspect ratio as the visible extent.

Now that we know how big our map will be, we can create and initialize our `mapnik.Map` object:

```
map = mapnik.Map(mapWidth, mapHeight)
map.background = mapnik.Color(BACKGROUND_COLOR)
```

We next need to define our various map styles, using a single style and rule for each of our map layers. Note that we use the various dictionary entries from our LAYERS list to define a map style for each layer:

```
for i,src in enumerate(LAYERS):
    style = mapnik.Style()
    rule = mapnik.Rule()

    if src['fillColor'] != None:
        symbol = mapnik.PolygonSymbolizer(
                    mapnik.Color(src['fillColor']))
        rule.symbols.append(symbol)
    if src['lineColor'] != None:
        symbol = mapnik.LineSymbolizer(
                    mapnik.Color(src['lineColor']),
                    src['lineWidth'])
        rule.symbols.append(symbol)
    if src['labelField'] != None:
        symbol = mapnik.TextSymbolizer(
                    mapnik.Expression(
                        "[" + src['labelField'] + "]"),
                    "DejaVu Sans Bold",
                    src['labelSize'],
                    mapnik.Color(src['labelColor']))
        symbol.allow_overlap = True
        rule.symbols.append(symbol)

    style.rules.append(rule)

    map.append_style("style-"+str(i+1), style)
```

We now need to define the various layers for our map:

```
for i,src in enumerate(LAYERS):
    layer = mapnik.Layer("layer-"+str(i+1))
    layer.datasource = mapnik.Shapefile(file=src['shapefile'])
    layer.styles.append("style-"+str(i+1))
    map.layers.append(layer)
```

Finally, we render the map image:

```
map.zoom_to_box(extent)
mapnik.render_to_file(map, "map.png", "png")
```

Since you have studied the various classes and methods in the *Learning Mapnik* section of this chapter, you should hopefully be able to understand what all this code does. If anything is unclear, please go back and review the relevant part of that section. A complete copy of this program can be downloaded as part of the source code available for this chapter.

Using the various constants we defined earlier, you should be able to use this program to draw the contents of the World Borders Dataset. Simply place the TM_WORLD_BORDERS-0.3 directory into the same folder as the shapeToMap.py program, and try running the program. All going well, the program should generate a map.png image, which displays the contents of the World Borders Dataset for Western and Central Europe:

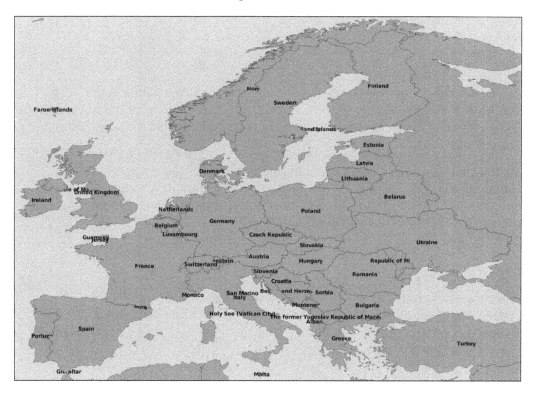

If you look closely at this image, you'll notice that some of the labels are hidden behind other polygons. This is because we have told our program to draw the polygons and their labels in the same map layer. To fix this, replace your LAYERS definition with the following:

```
LAYERS = [
    {'shapeFile' : "TM_WORLD_BORDERS-0.3/TM_WORLD_BORDERS-0.3.shp",
     'lineColor'  : "black",
     'lineWidth'  : 0.4,
     'fillColor'  : "#709070",
     'labelField' : None,
     'labelSize'  : None,
     'labelColor' : None,
    },
    {'shapeFile' : "TM_WORLD_BORDERS-0.3/TM_WORLD_BORDERS-0.3.shp",
     'lineColor'  : None,
     'lineWidth'  : None,
     'fillColor'  : None,
     'labelField' : "NAME",
     'labelSize'  : 12,
     'labelColor' : "black"
    }
]
```

As you can see, we're now displaying the shapefile in two separate map layers, one to draw the country polygons, and a second map layer to draw all the labels in front of the polygons. If you run your program again, you'll see that the labeling problem has been fixed.

This should give you an idea of how useful the shapeToMap.py program can be. Simply by changing the constants at the top of the program, you can quickly view the contents of any shapefile. In fact, many of the illustrations in this book were generated using a modified version of this program.

Next steps

While the shapeToMap.py program has been kept deliberately simple to make it easier to understand, there is a lot that can be done to improve this program and make it more useful. You might like to try challenging yourself by implementing the following new features:

- Add an optional labelHalo entry to each map layer, which is used to draw a halo around the label text.

- Add a labelPlacement entry to the map layer, to make it easy to control the label placement options.

- Add a `labelAllowOverlap` entry to the map layer, which controls whether or not the labels are allowed to overlap.

- Add a `filter` entry to the map layer, which is used to build a `mapnik.Filter()` expression to limit the set of features displayed within the map layer.

- Add an option to dynamically calculate the visible extent of the map based on the bounding box for each feature. This would allow you to generate the map without having to calculate the bounds beforehand.

- Add a call to `os.system("open map.png")` (for Mac OS X) or `os.startfile("map.png")` (for MS Windows) to automatically display the image once it has been generated.

- Add support for shapefiles which use a projection other than the default EPSG 4326.

- Load the configuration constants from a separate module, so you don't have to edit the Python source file every time you want to change the data to be displayed.

A more sophisticated version of `shapeToMap.py` called `generateMap.py` has been provided as part of the source code for this chapter. The `generateMap.py` program implements all of the preceding suggestions.

Summary

In this chapter, we covered the Mapnik map-generation library and how to use it within a Python program to create great-looking maps. You installed Mapnik, looked at a simple example of how it could be used, and then began to learn more about the process of constructing and styling a map.

We then examined Mapnik in more detail, looking at the various types of datasources which you can use to load spatial data into a map layer. We also examined the various symbolizers which can be used to display spatial features, how the visible extent is used to control the portion of the map to be displayed, and how to render a map as an image file. We then created a useful Python program called `shapeToMap.py`, which can be used to generate a map out of any spatial data stored in shapefiles, and finally looked at some of the ways in which `shapeToMap.py` could be improved to make it even more useful.

In the next chapter, we will look at various tools and techniques for analyzing spatial data, including how to use Python to solve a variety of interesting geospatial problems.

5
Analyzing Geospatial Data

In this chapter, we will look at the process of analyzing geospatial data. Sometimes, the results of your geospatial analysis will be one or more numbers, for example, *How many countries lie south of the Equator?* or *What is the length of the Australian coastline?* At other times, the results of your analysis will be a geometry object, for example, *Where is the northernmost point in Alaska?* or *What part of Texas lies east of New Mexico?* And at other times, the results of your analysis will be a list, for example, *Which countries are within 1,000 kilometers of New Guinea?* In all these cases, you will need to be familiar with the tools and techniques available for calculating your desired results.

To help you learn these tools and techniques, we will examine the following:

- How to install and use two powerful Python libraries for solving geospatial problems
- How to calculate and work with locations
- How to calculate the length of a LineString geometry in real-world units
- How to calculate the area of a Polygon using real-world units
- How to use a shapefile containing roads to build an abstract model of connected LineString geometries, and then use that model to calculate the shortest path between two points.

Let's start by looking at some of the Python libraries you can use for geospatial analysis.

Libraries for spatial analysis

You already have a couple of libraries that are useful for analyzing geospatial data: the OGR library includes methods for comparing and manipulating geometries, and Shapely is a wonderful library for working with and analyzing geometry data. There are, however, two other libraries that you will want to become familiar with: **PyProj**, which is a powerful library for calculating distances and locations on the Earth's surface, and **NetworkX**, which can build abstract mathematical models out of geospatial data and then analyze those models to solve various problems.

Let's take a closer look at these two libraries and install them both onto your computer.

PyProj

PyProj (`https://pypi.python.org/pypi/pyproj`) is a powerful tool for working with spatial reference systems using Python. PyProj itself is simply a Python interface to the PROJ.4 cartographic projection library, which is written in C. So, to install PyProj, you typically need to install the PROJ.4 library, and then install or build PyProj itself.

Before we get into the details of installing PyProj (and PROJ.4), let's look at what this library does and how it can be useful. If you remember from *Chapter 2, Geospatial Data*, a spatial reference system is a way of representing positions on the Earth's surface using coordinates. **Unprojected coordinates**, such as latitude and longitude values, directly represent a location on the Earth's surface by tracing a line from the center of the earth out to the desired point and then measuring the angle of that line in the east-west and north-south directions:

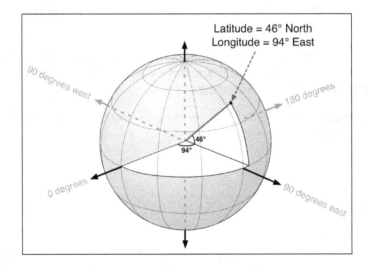

Projected coordinates, on the other hand, represent locations as positions on a two-dimensional Cartesian plane:

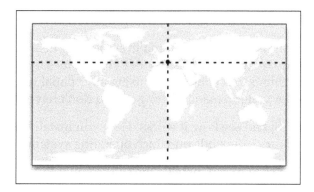

A spatial reference system, also known as a cartographic projection, is a way of translating from points on the Earth's surface to points on a two-dimensional plane. PROJ.4 (and also PyProj) is a tool for working with these projections.

It is vital that you know which map projection was used to generate your geospatial data. Using the wrong projection will ruin all your calculations and map visualizations. Map projections are also important because it is all-but-impossible to do spatial calculations using data in unprojected coordinate systems such as EPSG 4326. For example, imagine that you want to calculate the area of the following polygon, which represents the outline of Loch Ness in Scotland:

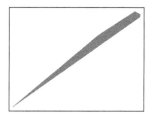

The coordinates for this polygon are in EPSG 4326 — that is, they are latitude and longitude values. If you wanted to, you could load this polygon into Shapely and ask it to calculate the area:

```
>>> wkt = "POLYGON ((-4.335556 57.373056,-4.676389 57.138611,-
4.447778 57.324722,-4.349167 57.386944,-4.334444 57.379444,-4.335556
57.373056))"
>>> polygon = shapely.wkt.loads(wkt)
>>> print polygon.area
0.006077434151
```

The result, however, is an *area in degrees*, which is a meaningless number. This is because Shapely doesn't know about spatial reference systems. It naively treats the latitude and longitude values as (x,y) coordinates, which means that spatial calculations like this cannot produce useful or accurate results.

What you actually want is the area measured in something meaningful, such as square meters or square miles. This is where PyProj comes in. PyProj allows you to perform calculations and conversions using any spatial reference system. PyProj does all the heavy mathematical lifting so you don't have to.

Now, let's install PyProj and see how it works. How you install PyProj (and the underlying PROJ.4 library), depends on which operating system you are using:

- For MS Windows, you can install a prebuilt copy of PyProj from `http://www.lfd.uci.edu/~gohlke/pythonlibs/#pyproj`. This installer includes PROJ.4, so you don't need to install it separately.

- For Mac OS X, you will need to do the following:

    1. Download and install the PROJ.4 library. A Mac installer for PROJ.4 can be downloaded from `http://www.kyngchaos.com/software/frameworks`.

    2. If you don't already have XCode installed on your computer, go to the Mac App store and download the latest version. XCode is Apple's development system, and can be downloaded for free.

    3. If you are using a version of Mac OS X less than 10.9 (Yosemite), you will need to separately install the command-line tools. To do this, start up XCode and choose the **Preferences...** command from the **XCode** menu. In the **Downloads** tab, there will be an option to install the command-line tools; enable this option and wait for the required tools to be installed.

 If you are using Mac OS X 10.9 (Yosemite) or later, you can skip this step.

4. Download the source code to PyProj from
   `https://pypi.python.org/pypi/pyproj`.

5. Using the terminal, `cd` into the PyProj directory you downloaded
   and type the following commands:

   ```
   python setup.py build
   sudo python.setup.py install
   ```

6. Finally, start up Python and try typing the following command:

   ```
   import pyproj
   ```

   The Python prompt should reappear without any error message.

- For Linux, you can either use your favorite package manager to install
  PROJ.4 and then PyProj, or else you can build them both from source by
  following the instructions available at `http://trac.osgeo.org/proj`
  and `https://github.com/jswhit/pyproj`.

Now that you have installed PyProj, let's see how the library can be used. There are
two main classes provided by PyProj:

- **Proj**: This class represents a spatial projection, and allows you to convert
  coordinates, either singly or en masse, between projections

- **Geod**: This is a *geodetic computation* class that allows you to perform various
  calculations based on coordinates that use a given spatial reference system

Let's see how PyProj can be used to calculate the distance between two points.
Open up a terminal window, start up your Python interpreter, and enter the
following code:

```
import pyproj
geod = pyproj.Geod(ellps="WGS84")
lat1 = -38.137
long1 = 176.349
lat2 = -41.286
long2 = 174.776
heading1,heading2,distance = geod.inv(long1, lat1, long2, lat2)
print int(distance)
```

The two coordinates represent the locations of the cities of Rotorua and Wellington, in New Zealand:

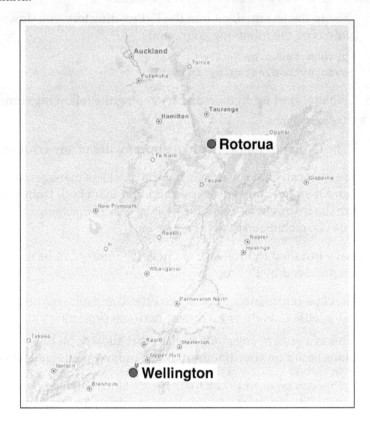

All going well, you should see the number 374,729 printed out, which is the as-the-crow-flies (great circle) distance between these two cities, measured in meters.

Notice that we use `ellps="WGS84"` to set the spatial reference system for our Geod object. This value sets the mathematical model for the shape of the Earth to be used by the geodetic calculator – WGS84 is the name for the ellipsoid used by the EPSG 4326 spatial reference system, so we are effectively telling PyProj that the coordinates are measured in latitude and longitude.

PyProj can also be used to convert between coordinate systems. We will look at this shortly, when we see how it can be combined with Shapely to perform accurate spatial calculations.

NetworkX

NetworkX is a Python library for defining and analyzing mathematical **graphs**. In mathematical terms, a graph is a collection of **vertices** joined together by **edges**:

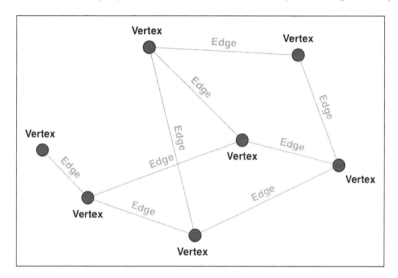

Each edge is typically assigned a value, called a **weight**, which can be used to perform queries against the graph. Each edge can be **directed**—that is, you can only follow the edge in one direction—or it can be undirected, allowing you to follow the edge in either direction.

While these graphs are an interesting mathematical concept, they are also useful for geospatial analysis because you can use a graph to represent locations and the ways of moving between them. For example, the vertices may represent towns, while the edges may represent roads that connect these various towns together. When used in this way, the edges are usually weighted by how long the road is, so that longer roads have a greater weight, and the entire graph can be used to calculate the shortest path between two points.

NetworkX is a very powerful library for working with mathematical graphs. Even better, it includes the ability to read a shapefile and convert it into a graph. This allows you to very simply convert geospatial data into an abstract graph representation, which you can then use to analyze the relationship between locations in various useful ways.

 In NetworkX, the vertices in a graph are called **nodes**.

Let's go ahead and install the NetworkX library now. The main website for NetworkX can be found at `https://networkx.github.io`, and you can download the library directly from `https://pypi.python.org/pypi/networkx`.

Since NetworkX is written in pure Python, you can simply download the source code and then type `python setup.py install` to install it into your `site-packages` directory, or if you prefer you can install it using pip by typing `pip install networkx`.

For more details, refer to the NetworkX installation instructions, which can be found at `http://networkx.github.io/documentation/latest/install.html`.

Once you have installed NetworkX, check that it works by typing the following into the Python command prompt:

```
import networkx

graph = networkx.Graph()
graph.add_edge("New York", "San Francisco", weight=2908)
graph.add_edge("San Francisco", "Los Angeles", weight=382)
graph.add_edge("Los Angeles", "New York", weight=2776)
graph.add_edge("San Francisco", "Portland", weight=635)

print networkx.shortest_path(graph, "New York", "Portland")
```

This simple program builds a NetworkX graph where the nodes represent cities and the edges represent roads connecting those cities. For each edge, the weight represents the driving distance in miles between those two cities. Using this simple graph, we then ask NetworkX to show us the shortest path between New York and Portland in Oregon.

All going well, running the preceding code will tell you that the shortest path is to go from New York to San Francisco, and from there to Portland:

```
['New York', 'San Francisco', 'Portland']
```

Obviously, there is a lot more you can do with NetworkX, and we will be using this library later in this chapter. For the moment, however, it's enough to know that you can use NetworkX to build an abstract graph out of your spatial data, and then use the NetworkX analysis functions to calculate useful information based on your graph.

Spatial analysis recipes

Now that we have a full set of geospatial analysis libraries available to us, let's see how we can use them to solve some real-world problems. We will look at how we can calculate and work with locations, lengths, and areas, as well as how we can use NetworkX to calculate the shortest available path between two points.

Calculating and comparing coordinates

As we saw earlier, PyProj can be used to calculate the real-world distance between two locations. It can also be used to measure the angle of a line going between two points, and calculate new points based on a starting point, a distance, and a heading.

Let's use PyProj to calculate the distance between two points. We will then use it to calculate a location at a certain distance and heading from a given point.

Start by creating a new Python program named `coord_analysis.py`. Enter the following code into the start of this program:

```
import pyproj
geod = pyproj.Geod(ellps="WGS84")
```

So far, this is identical to the code we saw earlier: we simply import the PyProj library and create a geodetic calculation object based on the WGS84 ellipsoid. If you remember, this is the mathematical model of the Earth's surface that is used by the standard EPSG 4326 spatial reference system.

We are now going to add some code to prompt the user to enter the desired coordinates. This is all standard Python code, and should not require any further explanation:

```
def get_coord(prompt):
    while True:
        s = raw_input(prompt + " (lat,long): ")
        if "," not in s: continue
        s1,s2 = s.split(",", 1)
        try:
            latitude = float(s1.strip())
        except ValueError:
            continue
        try:
            longitude = float(s2.strip())
        except ValueError:
            continue
        return latitude,longitude
```

```
lat1,long1 = get_coord("Starting coordinate")
lat2,long2 = get_coord("Ending coordinate")
```

Now that we have the two sets of latitude and longitude values, we can use PyProj to calculate the actual distance between these two points:

```
heading1,heading2,distance = geod.inv(long1, lat1, long2, lat2)
```

This is exactly the same code that we saw earlier. The `geod.inv()` method takes the two coordinates and returns the *heading* (the angle in degrees of a line from the first point to the second point, measured clockwise from due north), the *inverse heading* (the angle of a line from the second point back to the first point, again measured clockwise from due north), and the *distance* (measured in meters) between the two points.

Notice that the call to `geod.inv()` requires us to supply the longitude value before the latitude value. This is because PyProj works with any coordinate system, and the longitude represents the x (left-to-right) value, while the latitude represents the y (bottom-to-top) value. The x value is always listed first when dealing with generic coordinates that could be in any spatial reference system.

Now that we have calculated these three numbers, let's display them so that the user can see the results of our calculation:

```
print "Heading = %0.2f degrees" % heading1
print "Inverse heading = %0.2f degrees" % heading2
print "Distance = %0.2f kilometers" % (distance/1000)
```

To check it out, save your program and run it in a terminal window. Then enter the following coordinates into your program:

```
Starting coordinate: 37.774929, -122.419416
Ending coordinate: 34.052234, -118.243685
```

These two coordinates represent the locations of San Francisco and Los Angeles. Assuming that you have entered the program correctly, the following results should be displayed:

```
Heading = 136.38 degrees
Inverse heading = -41.17 degrees
Distance = 559.04 kilometers
```

This tells us that if we were in a plane directly above downtown San Francisco and flew 559 kilometers at a heading of 136.38 degrees (measured clockwise from due north), you would end up in downtown Los Angeles. Similarly, if you were in Los Angeles and headed 559 kilometers at a heading of -41.17 degrees (again measured clockwise from due north), you would end up in San Francisco:

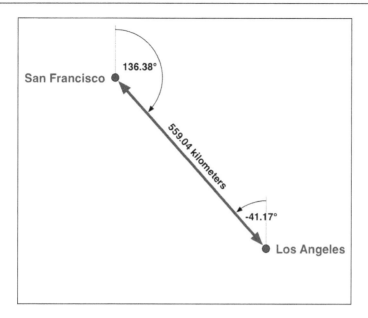

Now, let's add some code to calculate the coordinates for a point a certain distance and heading from an existing location. Comment out everything you wrote after the end of the get_coord() function, and then add the following to the end of your program:

```
def get_num(prompt):
    while True:
        s = raw_input(prompt + ": ")
        try:
            value = float(s)
        except ValueError:
            continue
        return value
```

This is a simple utility function to prompt the user to enter a numeric value. We will use this (along with the get_coord() function we wrote earlier) to prompt the user for the information we will need. Now add the following to the end of your program:

```
sLat,sLong = get_coord("Starting coordinate")
distance = get_num("Distance in kilometers") * 1000
heading = get_num("Heading")
```

Notice that we convert the distance measured in kilometers into the distance in meters—PyProj always works in meters, so we have to provide the distance in meters.

We are now ready to calculate the ending coordinate. Using PyProj, this is easy:

```
eLong,eLat,iHeading = geod.fwd(sLong, sLat, heading, distance)
```

The `geod.fwd()` method returns the desired coordinate (with the X value listed first), as well as the inverse heading. Our last task is to display these results to the user:

```
print "End point = (%0.4f,%0.4f)" % (eLat, eLong)
print "Inverse heading = %0.2f degrees" % iHeading
```

If you run this program, you can try entering a starting point, heading and distance, and the program will display the ending point. For example:

```
Starting coordinate (lat,long): 37.774929, -122.419416
Distance in kilometers: 559.04
Heading: 136.38
End point = (34.0521,-118.2440)
Inverse heading = -41.17 degrees
```

> The calculated end point is not quite the same as the value we saw earlier. This is because the distance and heading are only specified to two decimal degrees of accuracy.

Of course, for our program, we commented out the first calculation so we could concentrate on the second. An obvious improvement would be to add a simple text prompt asking the user which calculation to perform. But you can see how PyProj can be used to calculate and compare points on the Earth's surface—something that cannot be done easily when you use latitude and longitude values.

Calculating lengths

Now that we know how to calculate the distance (in meters) between two points, let's apply this technique to calculate the true length of any LineString geometry.

To calculate the total length of a LineString geometry, we need to split the LineString up into individual line segments, calculate the length of each line segment, and sum the result to get the total length of the entire LineString:

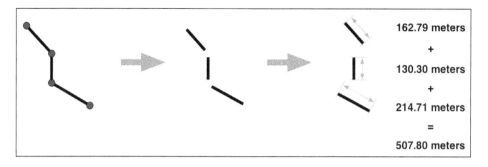

To see this in action, we need some LineString geometries to work with. For this example, we will use LineStrings representing the primary and secondary roads in California. This data can be downloaded from the US Census Bureau's website at `https://www.census.gov/geo/maps-data/data/tiger-line.html`. Scroll down to the section labeled **2014 TIGER/Line Shapefiles**, and click on the **Download** option, then click on **Web interface**. From the download page, choose **Roads** from the **Select a layer type** drop-down menu, and then click on the **Submit** button. Finally, choose **California** from the **Primary and Secondary Roads** drop-down menu, and click on the **Download** button to download the required data.

The resulting shapefile will be in a compressed ZIP archive named `tl_2014_06_prisecroads.zip`. Decompress this archive, and place the resulting shapefile somewhere convenient. Create a new file in the same directory as the shapefile with the name `calc_lengths.py`, and then enter the following code into this file:

```
import osgeo.ogr
import shapely.wkt
import pyproj

geod = pyproj.Geod(ellps="WGS84")

shapefile = osgeo.ogr.Open("tl_2014_06_prisecroads.shp")
layer = shapefile.GetLayer(0)

for i in range(layer.GetFeatureCount()):
    feature = layer.GetFeature(i)
    geometry = shapely.wkt.loads(
        feature.GetGeometryRef().ExportToWkt())
```

This should all be quite familiar to you—we just import the various libraries we will use, create a new `pyproj.Geod` object to use for our length calculations, and then iterate over the contents of the shapefile one feature at a time. As you can see, we use the `shapely.wkt.loads()` function to convert the feature into a Shapely geometry object.

Now that we have a Shapely geometry, our next task is to split that geometry into individual line segments and calculate the length of each segment. Let's do that:

```
tot_length = 0
prev_long,prev_lat = geometry.coords[0]
for cur_long,cur_lat in geometry.coords[1:]:
    heading1,heading2,distance = geod.inv(
        prev_long, prev_lat, cur_long, cur_lat)
    tot_length = tot_length + distance
    prev_long,prev_lat = cur_long,cur_lat
```

Because the Shapely geometry is a LineString, we can access the individual coordinates that make up the LineString using `geometry.coords`. We then process each pair of coordinates in turn, using the technique we learned earlier to calculate the distance in meters between the two coordinates. We keep track of the total calculated length across all the coordinate pairs, giving us the total length of the LineString geometry.

 If our road data had been in a projected coordinate system that preserved distances, we could have simply asked Shapely to calculate the total length of each LineString by accessing the `geometry.length` attribute. This won't work for EPSG 4326 data, however, because once again the results would be a length in degrees.

Our last task is to do something with the calculated length. Let's simply print it out, along with the name of the road:

```
print feature.GetField("FULLNAME"), int(tot_length)
```

In theory, our program should now work, so let's try running it:

```
$ python calc_lengths.py
N Wheeler Ridge Rd 1616
N Main St 1595
...
```

So far so good; as you can see, the total length of each road, in meters, is being calculated. Unfortunately, if we wait a few more seconds, our program will raise a Python exception and stop:

```
Traceback (most recent call last):
  File "calc_lengths.py", line 23, in <module>
    prev_long,prev_lat = geometry.coords[0]
  File "/Library/Frameworks/GEOS.framework/Versions/3/Python/2.7/shapely/
geometry/base.py", line 634, in coords
```

```
    "Multi-part geometries do not provide a coordinate sequence")
NotImplementedError: Multi-part geometries do not provide a coordinate
sequence
```

What's going on here? It seems that `geometry.coords` is not available because the geometry is not an ordinary LineString. Indeed, if you remember from *Chapter 2, Geospatial Data*, shapefiles make no distinction between simple geometries and collections of those geometries, so a LineString in the shapefile might actually be a collection of LineStrings. This is exactly what is happening in this case—if you were to load the affected feature into memory using the interactive Python command prompt, you could print out the geometry type to see what is wrong:

```
>>> geometry =
shapely.wkt.loads(feature.GetGeometryRef().ExportToWkt())
>>> print geometry.geom_type
MultiLineString
```

So we have a road represented by a MultiLineString geometry rather than a LineString geometry. Fortunately, it's easy to split apart a MultiLineString and process the individual LineStrings one at a time. Here is what our entire program looks like once we add this feature:

```
import osgeo.ogr
import shapely.wkt
import pyproj

geod = pyproj.Geod(ellps="WGS84")

shapefile = osgeo.ogr.Open("tl_2014_06_prisecroads.shp")
layer = shapefile.GetLayer(0)

for i in range(layer.GetFeatureCount()):
    feature = layer.GetFeature(i)
    geometry = shapely.wkt.loads(
        feature.GetGeometryRef().ExportToWkt())

    lineStrings = []
    if geometry.geom_type == "LineString":
        lineStrings.append(geometry)
    elif geometry.geom_type == "MultiLineString":
        for lineString in geometry:
            lineStrings.append(lineString)

    tot_length = 0
```

```
for lineString in lineStrings:
    prev_long,prev_lat = lineString.coords[0]
    for cur_long,cur_lat in lineString.coords[1:]:
        heading1,heading2,distance = geod.inv(
            prev_long, prev_lat, cur_long, cur_lat)
        tot_length = tot_length + distance
        prev_long,prev_lat = cur_long,cur_lat

    print feature.GetField("FULLNAME"), int(tot_length)
```

Using this technique, we can calculate the exact length, in meters, for any linear geometry such as a LineString or MultiLineString. Indeed, we could even use the same technique to calculate the perimeter of a polygon geometry, by accessing the polygon's exterior linear ring and then processing it as if it were a LineString:

```
lineString = polygon.exterior
```

Calculating areas

In *Chapter 2, Geospatial Data*, we saw how we can calculate the area of a polygon using OGR and the World Mollweide projection (EPSG 54009). World Mollweide is an equal-area map projection that is reasonably accurate worldwide, and so is useful for calculating areas in square meters.

Instead of using OGR, let's apply the same technique using Shapely. The advantage of doing this is that we'll have access to all of Shapely's functionality, allowing us to manipulate and measure geometries in all sorts of useful ways. To do this, we will make use of a handy Shapely function called `shapely.ops.transform()`. This lets you apply a transformation function to every coordinate within a geometry. The transformation can be anything you want (you can write your own transformation function in Python if you want), but most importantly, you can use PyProj to implement a transformation function that converts from EPSG 4326 to ESPG 54009 so that you can accurately calculate the area for any geometry.

Let's see how this works. Place a copy of the TM_WORLD_BORDERS-0.3 shapefile you downloaded earlier into a convenient directory, and create a new file named calc_areas.py in the same directory. Then enter the following code into this new file:

```
import osgeo.ogr
import shapely.wkt
import shapely.ops
import pyproj
```

```
shapefile = osgeo.ogr.Open("TM_WORLD_BORDERS-0.3.shp")
layer = shapefile.GetLayer(0)

src_proj = pyproj.Proj(proj="longlat", ellps="WGS84",
datum="WGS84")
dst_proj = pyproj.Proj(proj="moll", lon_0=0, x_0=0, y_0=0,
ellps="WGS84", datum="WGS84", units="m")

def latlong_to_mollweide(longitude, latitude):
    return pyproj.transform(src_proj, dst_proj,
                            longitude, latitude)

for i in range(layer.GetFeatureCount()):
    feature = layer.GetFeature(i)
    wkt = feature.getGeometryRef().ExportToWkt()
    geometry = shapely.wkt.loads(wkt)

    transformed = shapely.ops.transform(latlong_to_mollweide,
                                        geometry)
    area = int(transformed.area/1000000)

    print feature.GetField("NAME"), area
```

As you can see, we have defined a transformation function, `latlong_to_mollweide()`, that converts a given latitude and longitude value into an (x,y) coordinate in the Mollweide coordinate reference system. Mollweide is based on meters, so Shapely can then perform calculations against that geometry and return a result in meters.

When you run the `calc_areas.py` program, you should see a list of countries and the area of the associated polygons in the World Borders Dataset, measured in square kilometers:

```
$ python calc_areas.py
Antigua and Barbuda 546
Algeria 2326137
Azerbaijan 86014
Albania 28702
...
```

The great thing about using `shapely.ops.transform()` is that you can use all of Shapely's calculative and geometry-manipulation features on the resulting geometries. For example, New Zealand has an exclusive economic zone that extends 200 miles out from the coastline. Using the `buffer()` method, you could calculate the shape of this exclusive economic zone by expanding the outline of New Zealand to include all points within 200 miles of the coastline:

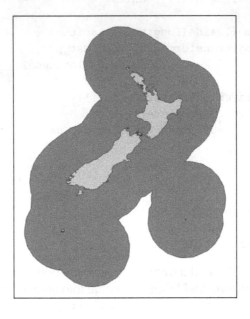

Buffering is an extremely powerful operation. For example, you can use `buffer()` along with the `intersects()` method to identify all countries within a given distance of a starting geometry. For example:

```
buffered_area = test_country['geom'].buffer(1000000)
for country in countries:
    if country['geom'].intersects(buffered_area):
        print "%s is within 1000 km of %s" %
(country['name'], test_country['name'])
```

Calculating shortest paths

For our final example, we will take a shapefile containing road data and use it to calculate the shortest path between two points. This is a fairly complex example employing various techniques for analyzing and manipulating geometry data. It also uses the NetworkX library to perform the shortest path calculation on an abstract representation of the road network.

Let's start by looking at how NetworkX converts a shapefile containing LineString geometries into an abstract network. If you were to look at a small part of the `tl_2014_06_prisecroads` shapefile, you would see what appears to be a connected series of roads, for example:

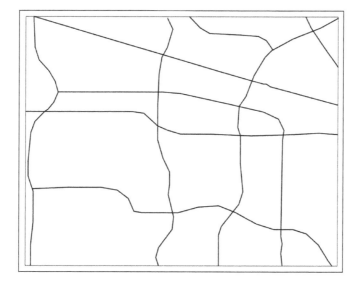

However, the roads don't actually stop where they intersect—the road features simply continue on, overlapping other roads as necessary. On the map, these may look like intersections, but there is no real intersection point where two roads meet or cross:

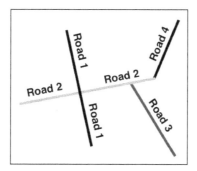

This is important because of the way NetworkX converts LineString geometries into an abstract graph—NetworkX will think that two LineStrings intersect if and only if they have identical starting or ending points; simply crossing over does not mean that the two roads intersect. In the preceding example, **Road 2** and **Road 4** will be the only roads that are considered to be connected—even though **Road 2** appears to intersect with **Road 1** and **Road 3**, the lack of matching endpoints means that these roads will be excluded from the graph.

To allow NetworkX to convert the road shapefile into a network, we need to split the roads at the points where they intersect:

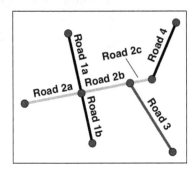

Mathematically speaking, this is known as generating a **planar graph** out of the network of overlapping roads. This process is not perfect—it ignores places where bridges and viaducts, not to mention *Do Not Enter* signs, prevent a traveler from taking a particular turnoff. However, converting the road shapefile into a planar graph is a good starting point, and you can always exclude particular intersections from the calculation if you have a list of bridges and other no-entry points.

Let's go ahead and convert our road shapefile into a planar graph. To do this, create a new Python program called `split_roads.py`, and enter the following code into this file:

```python
import os
import os.path
import shutil
import osgeo.ogr
import osgeo.osr
import shapely.wkt

SRC_SHAPEFILE = "tl_2014_06_prisecroads.shp"

all_roads = []
shapefile = osgeo.ogr.Open(SRC_SHAPEFILE)
```

```
layer = shapefile.GetLayer(0)
for i in range(layer.GetFeatureCount()):
    feature = layer.GetFeature(i)
    wkt = feature.GetGeometryRef().ExportToWkt()
    geometry = shapely.wkt.loads(wkt)
    all_roads.append(geometry)
```

Apart from the extra `import` statements (which we will need shortly), this code should be fairly clear: we're simply loading the LineString geometries from our `tl_2014_06_prisecroads.shp` shapefile into the `all_roads` list.

> If your shapefile is in a different directory, edit the `SRC_SHAPEFILE` constant so that the program can find the shapefile.

Our next task is to split the roads up at the intersection points. Fortunately, Shapely makes this quite easy. Add the following to the end of your program:

```
split_roads = []

for i in range(len(all_roads)):
    cur_road = all_roads[i]
    crossroads = []
    for j in range(len(all_roads)):
        if i == j: continue
        other_road = all_roads[j]
        if cur_road.crosses(other_road):
            crossroads.append(other_road)
    if len(crossroads) > 0:
        for other_road in crossroads:
            cur_road = cur_road.difference(other_road)
        if cur_road.geom_type == "MultiLineString":
            for split_road in cur_road.geoms:
                split_roads.append(split_road)
        elif cur_road.geom_type == "LineString":
            split_roads.append(cur_road)
    else:
        split_roads.append(cur_road)
```

As you can see, we identify any roads that cross the current road by calling Shapely's `crosses()` method. We then use the `difference()` method to remove each crossroad from the current road; this has the effect of splitting the road up at the point where the other road crosses it:

Finally, we want to save the split roads back into a shapefile. To do this, add the following code to the end of your program:

```
driver = osgeo.ogr.GetDriverByName("ESRI Shapefile")
if os.path.exists("split_roads"):
    shutil.rmtree("split_roads")
os.mkdir("split_roads")
dstFile = driver.CreateDataSource("split_roads/split_roads.shp")

spatialReference = osgeo.osr.SpatialReference()
spatialReference.SetWellKnownGeogCS("WGS84")

layer = dstFile.CreateLayer("Layer", spatialReference)

for road in split_roads:
    wkt = shapely.wkt.dumps(road)
    linestring = osgeo.ogr.CreateGeometryFromWkt(wkt)

    feature = osgeo.ogr.Feature(layer.GetLayerDefn())
    feature.SetGeometry(linestring)

    layer.CreateFeature(feature)
    feature.Destroy()

dstFile.Destroy()
```

This code should be familiar to you, as we used the same technique in *Chapter 2, Geospatial Data*, when we looked at how to write vector data into a shapefile. The only new thing here is the fact that we're using `shutil.rmtree()` followed by `os.mkdir()` to delete and then re-create the directory in which we store the shapefile; this allows us to run the program again without having to remember to delete the shapefile each time.

This completes our `split_roads.py` program. It will take a few minutes to split all 8,000 roads in the `tl_2014_06_prisecroads` shapefile, so just leave it running as you start working on the next program.

Once we have the set of split roads, we'll want to have another program which uses them to calculate the shortest path between two points. Let's start writing that program now. We'll call this program `calc_shortest_path.py`. Create this file, and enter the following code into it:

```
import shapely.wkt
import pyproj
import networkx
```

We are now going to write some utility functions which we'll need to do the shortest-path calculation. First off, we'll use the technique we saw earlier to calculate the distance in meters between two points:

```
def calc_distance(lat1, long1, lat2, long2):
    geod = pyproj.Geod(ellps="WGS84")
    heading1,heading2,distance = geod.inv(long1, lat1, long2,
lat2)
    return distance
```

We will use this function to write another function that calculates the total length of a LineString geometry:

```
def calc_length(linestring):
    tot_length = 0
    prev_long,prev_lat = linestring.coords[0]
    for cur_long,cur_lat in linestring.coords[1:]:
        distance = calc_distance(prev_lat, prev_long,
                                 cur_lat, cur_long)
        tot_length = tot_length + distance
        prev_long,prev_lat = cur_long,cur_lat
    return int(tot_length)
```

Next, we will need a copy of the `get_coord()` function we wrote earlier:

```
def get_coord(prompt):
    while True:
        s = raw_input(prompt + " (lat,long): ")
        if "," not in s: continue
        s1,s2 = s.split(",", 1)
        try:
            latitude = float(s1.strip())
        except ValueError:
```

```
            continue
        try:
            longitude = float(s2.strip())
        except ValueError:
            continue
        return latitude,longitude
```

There is one more function that we need to write: `find_closest_node`. This will find the node within a NetworkX graph that is closest to a given latitude and longitude value. We will need this to identify the starting and ending nodes for the shortest-path calculation.

Here is the code for the `find_closest_node` function, which you should add to the end of your program:

```
def find_closest_node(graph, latitude, longitude):
    closest_node = None
    min_distance = None
    for node in graph.nodes():
        distance = calc_distance(node[1], node[0],
                                 latitude, longitude)
        if closest_node == None:
            closest_node = node
            min_distance = distance
        elif distance < min_distance:
            closest_node = node
            min_distance = distance
    return closest_node
```

To find the closest node, we simply go through all the nodes (vertices) in the graph and calculate the distance in meters between the node and the desired coordinate. We then select and return the node with the smallest distance.

We are now ready to start writing the main part of our program. The first step is to ask NetworkX to read the `split_roads` shapefile and create a graph out of the road data:

```
graph = networkx.read_shp("split_roads/split_roads.shp")
```

This reads through the shapefile and generates a NetworkX graph, where each edge represents a road and each node represents the endpoint of a road. Because NetworkX has no way of knowing how a road or endpoint should be identified, it uses the latitude and longitude to identify each endpoint (that is, each node), and the starting and ending latitude and longitude to identify each road (that is, each edge). Thus, the resulting graph will consist of nodes and edges that look something like the following diagram:

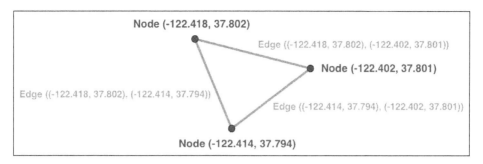

The resulting graph will be quite large, as there are almost 10,000 roads to be imported from our shapefile.

Our next task might seem a bit odd: because there is no guarantee that every road can be reached from every other road, we need to reduce the graph down to just the reachable set of roads. If we don't do this, our shortest-path calculation is likely to fail. To remove the unreachable roads, we use the `connected_component_subgraphs()` function to identify the portion of the graph which contains the largest number of connected roads, and use this subgraph for the shortest-path calculation. Here is the necessary code:

```
graph = networkx.connected_component_subgraphs
(graph.to_undirected()).next()
```

Note that, because the `connected_component_subgraphs()` function requires an undirected graph, while the `read_shp()` function returns a directed graph, we have to use the `to_undirected()` method to make the graph undirected.

> If you get a `'list' object has no attribute 'next'` error, you may be using a different version of NetworkX. In this case, replace this line with `graph = networkx.connected_component_subgraphs(graph.to_undirected())[0]`.

Now that we have the useable set of roads, our next task is to calculate the length of each of these roads. This length value will be used as the basis for the shortest-path calculation. Fortunately, the length calculation is quite straightforward:

```
for node1,node2 in graph.edges():
    wkt = graph[node1][node2]['Wkt']
    linestring = shapely.wkt.loads(wkt)
    length = calc_length(linestring)
    graph.edge[node1][node2]['length'] = length
```

As you can see, we extract the original LineString geometry for each edge, in WKT format, and then use that to create a Shapely geometry object. We then use our `calc_length()` function to calculate the total length of the road and store the resulting value as a `length` attribute into the edge. Running this code will calculate and store the length for every road in the graph.

With this done, we are finally ready to calculate the shortest path. We start by asking the user to enter the latitude and longitude values for the desired start and end points:

```
start_lat, start_long = get_coord("Starting Coordinate")
end_lat, end_long = get_coord("Ending Coordinate")
```

The values entered by the user define two coordinates; we need to use these to identify the starting and ending nodes. We can do this using the `find_closest_node()` function we wrote earlier:

```
start_node = find_closest_node(graph, start_lat, start_long)
end_node   = find_closest_node(graph, end_lat, end_long)
```

Now we can get the shortest path between the two nodes, based on the length values we calculated earlier:

```
path = networkx.shortest_path(graph, start_node, end_node,
    "length")
```

The returned `path` value is a list of the nodes that make up the shortest path. Let's finish our program by printing out the details of this path:

```
tot_length = 0
prev_node = path[0]
for cur_node in path[1:]:
    edge = graph.edge[prev_node][cur_node]
    print (str(prev_node) + " -> " + str(cur_node) +
            ", length = " + str(edge['length']))
    tot_length = tot_length + edge['length']
    prev_node = cur_node
print "Total length = " + str(tot_length)
```

Now that we've completed the program, let's test it out. Run the `calc_shortest_path.py` script. The program will start by loading the road network into memory and calculating the length for each road:

```
$ python calc_shortest_path.py
Loading road network into memory...
graph has 7976 nodes and 9709 edges
Calculating road lengths...
```

After the lengths are calculated, the program will then prompt you for the desired starting and ending coordinates. Let's enter the coordinates for Oakland and San Louis Obespo, which are both cities within California:

```
Starting Coordinate (lat,long): 37.794189, -122.276469
Ending Coordinate (lat,long): 35.281107, -120.661211
```

The program will then calculate the nearest matching nodes, and the shortest path between these two points:

```
start node = (-122.272515, 37.797457)
end node = (-120.66285, 35.285892)
(-122.272515, 37.797457) -> (-122.176834, 37.719054), length = 12528
(-122.176834, 37.719054) -> (-122.176734, 37.718964), length = 13
...
(-120.663604, 35.286751) -> (-120.663466, 35.286594), length = 21
(-120.663466, 35.286594) -> (-120.66285, 35.285892), length = 95
Total length = 358838
```

Of course, printing out the latitude and longitude of each endpoint like this isn't particularly useful—it would be much nicer for the user if we displayed the shortest path on a map. If you wanted to, you could save the calculated path into a shapefile and then use Mapnik to display the contents of that shapefile as part of a map. But you can see how the shortest path calculation works, and what's required to get road data into a format that NetworkX can work with.

Summary

In this chapter, you learned about two new useful libraries for analyzing geospatial data. We then looked at various techniques for manipulating and analyzing spatial data, including ways of accurately calculating distances, lengths, locations, and areas.

Next, we looked at how to convert intersecting roads into a planar graph, which we stored in a shapefile so that we could perform a shortest-path calculation based on the road data. Finally, we wrote a program to calculate the shortest path between any two points. As we worked through these various problems, we learned a number of techniques for manipulating and analyzing geospatial data—techniques which you will use regularly when you write your own programs for geospatial analysis.

In the next chapter, we will bring together everything you have learned to implement a complete geospatial analysis system using Python.

6
Building a Complete Geospatial Analysis System

In this chapter, we will take the skills we have learned in the previous chapters and apply them to build a suite of programs that solve a complicated geospatial problem. In doing so, we will learn:

- What map matching is, and how it works
- How to use map matching to generate a heatmap of roads traveled based on GPS recordings
- How to download road map data and transform it into a network of roads
- How to store the road network in a database
- How to generate your own records of journeys using a GPS tracking device
- How to implement a map matching algorithm to match GPS recordings to an existing road network, and use the results to calculate how often each road segment was used
- How to generate a great-looking GPS Heatmap using this calculated data

Let's start by examining the concept of map matching, and see how it can be useful in solving various geospatial problems.

Matching GPS data against a map

A GPS recording device captures a series of latitude and longitude coordinates over time. As the device is carried by someone moving from place to place, the GPS coordinates record the person's movements. The following map shows a typical GPS recording:

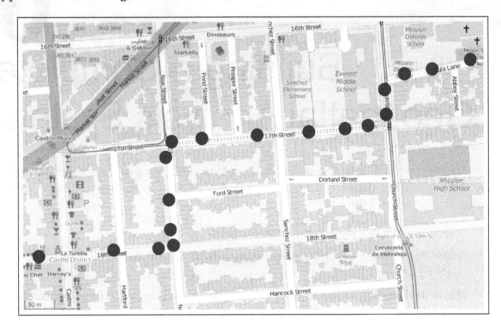

GPS devices are relatively cheap and remarkably accurate, allowing you to record a journey taken on foot, by bicycle, car, or truck. However, by itself, all the GPS device is doing is recording a series of coordinates—the GPS device doesn't know which roads you followed on your journey.

Map matching is the process of taking a GPS recording and matching it against a database of roads to identify which set of roads were used on that journey. For map matching to be successful, you need three things:

- An accurate GPS recording of the journey, including enough GPS coordinates to identify which roads were taken.

- An accurate database of roads.

- A suitable algorithm to match the GPS coordinates against the road database.

Once you know which roads were taken, you can use this information for various purposes. For example, a turn-by-turn navigation system will use its knowledge of the road database and the path taken so far to suggest the next turn to take.

You can also use map matching for historical purposes: keeping track of which routes a traveler took on their journey, possibly to optimize future journeys, or noting which roads were most commonly traveled.

In this chapter, we will implement a complete map matching system, using an appropriate database of road data and a sophisticated algorithm for matching a GPS recording against those roads. We will use this information to generate a heatmap of commonly-used roads over a series of historical GPS recordings.

An overview of the GPS Heatmap system

The system we are implementing will be called the **GPS Heatmap**. We will download a set of road data and convert this data into a network of directed road segments. We will then either generate or download a collection of GPS recordings from various journeys, which we will use to identify commonly-traveled roads. Finally, we will generate a heatmap based on how often the roads are traveled, providing a visual summary of the most commonly-traveled roads captured by the GPS device. The resulting output will look something like the following:

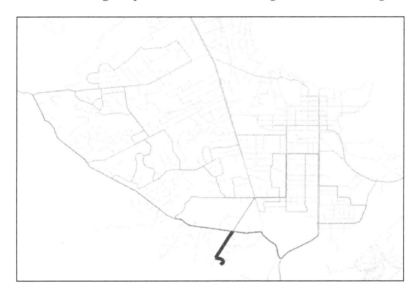

A heatmap typically uses a color gradient ranging from blue to red to draw the roads, with blue used for the less-traveled roads and red for the most commonly traveled roads. In the printed edition of this book, however, the heatmaps will appear in black and white, so we have selected a single shade of blue so that the heatmap still makes sense when printed.

To allow our GPS Heatmap program to work as efficiently as possible, we will make use of a PostGIS database to store the underlying road data. We will generate a planar graph of the nonintersecting road segments, use this data to build a network of connected road segments, and store this network in the database for quick access. We will then use a map matching algorithm to calculate a **tally** for each road segment. These tallies then form the basis for generating the GPS heatmap image, with a suitable color chosen for each road segment based on the calculated tally for that segment.

Because our GPS Heatmap program consists of many parts, we will implement it as a suite of individual Python programs:

- `init_db.py`: This will initialize the PostGIS database, providing us with a place to store the data as we load and process it.

- `import_roads.py`: This will import the road data from a shapefile into the PostGIS database.

- `split_roads.py`: This will convert the imported roads into a series of nonoverlapping road segments by calculating a planar graph based on the raw road data.

- `calc_directed_network.py`: This will use the road segments to generate a directed network of connected road segments. This tells us how the various road segments are connected, and which segments lead off from a given point.

- `map_matcher.py`: This performs the actual map matching process, reading the raw GPS data from a GPX format file, using it to identify which road segments were traveled by the person using that GPS device, and incrementing the tally for each road segment as it is used.

- `generate_heatmap.py`: This will use the calculated tally data to generate a heatmap image for display.

Before we can start implementing these various programs, we will need to obtain the underlying data. Let's look at how to do this now.

Obtaining the necessary data

Your first choice is to decide which GPS dataset to use. You can capture your own GPS recordings using a GPS device if you wish, or you can make use of the GPS recordings provided with the example code for this chapter. Once you have decided which set of GPS data to use, you will need to download road data for the same area.

Let's start by deciding which set of GPS data you wish to use.

Obtaining GPS data

If you have your own GPS recording device, you might like to go out and capture your own GPS recordings as you travel back and forth in your local area. If you do not have your own GPS recording device, or if you do not want to capture your own GPS data, example GPS recordings are provided along with the sample code for this chapter.

These example recordings were taken in and around the author's home city of Rotorua, New Zealand. The recordings were captured using a Garmin Edge 500 cycle computer, and exported in GPX format. If you want to capture your own GPS recordings, make sure you record at least 20 separate journeys so that you have a good set of data to work with.

Not every GPS recording will be usable. Sometimes, the GPS data can be too inaccurate or might miss sections of your journey, leading to matching errors. Also, limitations in the map matching algorithm mean that any journey which U-turns along a road, or uses the same road segment twice, cannot be matched. For this reason, you may find that some of your recordings do not work.

Whether you use the sample recordings or create your own, place the resulting GPX format files into a directory named gps-data.

Downloading the road data

Once you have your GPS recordings, you next need a matching set of road data. If your GPS recordings were taken in the USA, you can use the TIGER data from the US Census Bureau's website. We used this site in the previous chapter to download all primary and secondary roads in California. In this case, you will want to download all the roads in your area. To do this:

1. Go to https://www.census.gov/geo/maps-data/data/tiger-line.html, scroll down to the section labeled **2014 TIGER/Line Shapefiles**, click on the **Download** option, and then click on **Web interface**.

2. From the download page, choose **Roads** from the **Select a layer type** drop-down menu, and then click on the **Submit** button.

3. Choose your state from the **All Roads** drop-down menu, and click on **Submit**.

4. You will then need to choose the county you are in, and finally you can click on the **Download** button to obtain the road data you need.

If you are outside the USA, you will need to find a suitable alternative. OpenStreetMap (`http://openstreetmap.org`) is one possible source of data, though you may need to hunt to find road data in a format you can use. Alternatively, the `https://koordinates.com` site might have data you can use.

If you want to make use of the example GPS recordings provided in this chapter, take the following steps:

1. Go to `https://koordinates.com`.

2. Click on the **Sign in** link in the upper-right-hand corner of the page.

3. Register for a free account by clicking on the **Register** link.

4. After signing in, you will see a map centered on your location. Pan the map over to New Zealand and zoom in on the central North Island until you find the city of Rotorua.

5. Click on the search box in the upper-left corner of the page, type `road centrelines` and press *Return*.

> Note the New Zealand spelling for the word "centrelines"; if you type `centerlines`, you won't find the data you're looking for.

6. The dataset you are looking for is called *Improved NZ Road Centrelines (August 2011)*. Click on the **+** icon beside this dataset, and the road data will appear on your map.

7. Next, zoom in further to show the city of Rotorua and its environs, click on the crop tool (⊡) in the upper-right-hand corner of the page, and drag out a rectangle that looks approximately like the following screenshot:

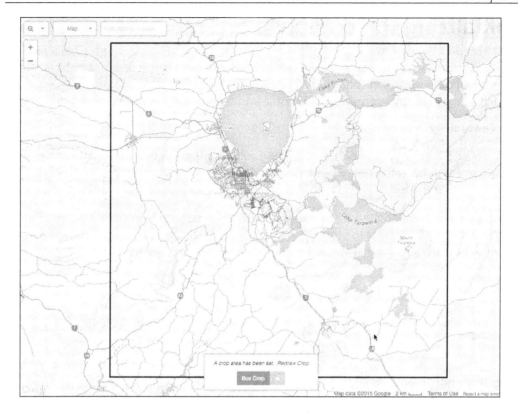

8. Once this has been selected, click on the **Download or Order** link in the upper-right-hand corner of the window. The default options (WGS 84 map projection and shapefile format) are exactly what you want, so just click on the **Accept terms and create download** button.

9. After a minute or so, the road data will be available for you to download. The resulting file will be named `kx-improved-nz-road-centrelines-august-2011-SHP.zip`. Decompress this ZIP archive, rename the resulting directory to `roads`, and place this directory somewhere convenient.

Implementing the GPS Heatmap system

Now that we have the necessary data, we're ready to start implementing our GPS Heatmap system. Create a directory named `gps-heatmap` to hold the suite of programs and their associated data files, and then place the two data directories you created earlier (`gps-data` and `roads`) into this directory.

We're now ready to start coding. Let's start by implementing the `init_db.py` program to initialize our PostGIS database.

Initializing the database

You should already have installed Postgres when you worked through *Chapter 3, Spatial Databases*. We're going to use Postgres to create and initialize a database to hold all our processed road data. The first step is to create the database itself, which you can do by typing the following into a terminal window:

```
% createdb gps_heatmap
```

This should create a database named `gps_heatmap`. If you get an authentication error, you will need to enter a password or use the `-U postgres` command-line option so that the `createdb` command can run.

Now that you have created the database itself, the next step is to turn it into a spatial database so we can use it to store geometry data. To do this, enter the following command into the terminal window:

```
% psql -d gps_heatmap -c "CREATE EXTENSION postgis;"
```

 Do not forget to add the `-U postgres` command-line option if you need it.

You have now created a spatial database for your Python code to use. We are now going to write the `init_db.py` script that initializes the various tables and indexes within this database. Go ahead and create the `init_db.py` file inside your main `gps-heatmap` directory, and enter the following code into this file:

```python
import psycopg2

connection = psycopg2.connect(database="gps_heatmap",
                              user="postgres")
cursor = connection.cursor()

cursor.execute("DROP TABLE IF EXISTS roads")
cursor.execute("CREATE TABLE roads (" +
               "id SERIAL PRIMARY KEY," +
               "name VARCHAR," +
               "centerline GEOMETRY)")
cursor.execute("CREATE INDEX ON roads USING GIST(centerline)")

connection.commit()
```

As you can see, we are using the `psycopg2` library to access our PostGIS database. We create a database connection and an associated `cursor` object. We then create the `roads` database table, first deleting it so that we can run this script again if we have to change the database structure.

 Don't forget to change the parameters to the `psycopg2.connect()` statement if you need to use a different username or password to access PostGIS on your computer.

The `roads` table will hold the raw road data imported from the shapefile that we have just downloaded. As you can see, this table will have three separate fields:

- `id`: This is the unique ID for this road in the database
- `name`: This is the name of the road
- `centerline`: This is a LineString geometry that represents the shape of this road

This is not the only database table we need, but it is enough to get us started. We will add more table definitions to the `init_db.py` program as we go along. For now, though, you should be able to run this program to create the `roads` table, which we will need in the next section when we import the downloaded road data into the database.

Importing the road data

We are now ready to import the road data from the downloaded shapefile into the database. The program that will do this is called `import_roads.py`. Go ahead and create this file, and enter the following Python code into it:

```python
import psycopg2
from osgeo import ogr

connection = psycopg2.connect(database="gps_heatmap",
                              user="postgres")
cursor = connection.cursor()

cursor.execute("DELETE FROM roads")
```

So far, all we have done is to open a connection to the database and delete the existing contents of the roads table. Next, we need to import the road data from the shapefile we downloaded. How we do this, of course, will vary depending on where the road data came from. For the *Improved NZ Road Centrelines* data, we will use the following code:

```
shapefile = ogr.Open("roads/improved-nz-road-centrelines-august-2011.
shp")
layer = shapefile.GetLayer(0)

for i in range(layer.GetFeatureCount()):
    feature = layer.GetFeature(i)
    geometry = feature.GetGeometryRef()

    if feature.GetField("descr") != None:
        name = feature.GetField("descr")
    elif feature.GetField("label") != None:
        name = feature.GetField("label")
    else:
        name = None

    centerline_wkt = geometry.ExportToWkt()

    cursor.execute("INSERT INTO roads (name, centerline) " +
                    "VALUES (%s, ST_GeomFromText(%s))",
                    (name, centerline_wkt))

connection.commit()
```

As you can see, we use OGR to import the road data from the shapefile, and use either the descr or the label field for the road name. This corresponds to the way the *NZ Road Centrelines* data has been defined, where sometimes the road name is in the descr field, and at other times the road name is in the label field. Some roads don't have a name (for example, where the road goes through a roundabout), and so in this case the road name will be set to None.

If you are using a different source of road data, you will need to modify this code to suit the way your road data is organized. Just make sure that you store the centerline and (where applicable) the name of the road into the roads table.

Splitting the road data into segments

As we have seen in the previous chapter, the points where roads touch or cross aren't automatically considered to be connection points for the purpose of building a road network. We first need to create a **planar graph** out of the intersecting roads, just like we did in the previous chapter. Our next task, therefore, is to split the roads up into segments, forming a planar graph of road segments out of the raw road data.

The `split_roads.py` program will split the raw road data into segments. Before we can write this program, however, we need to add a table to the database which will hold the road segments. To do this, add the following code to your `init_db.py` program, immediately before the call to `connection.commit()`:

```
cursor.execute("DROP TABLE IF EXISTS road_segments")
cursor.execute("CREATE TABLE road_segments (" +
               "id SERIAL PRIMARY KEY," +
               "name VARCHAR," +
               "centerline GEOMETRY," +
               "tally INTEGER)")
cursor.execute("CREATE INDEX ON road_segments USING GIST(centerline)")
```

As you can see, we create a new table called `road_segments` to hold the various segments in our planar graph. Each road segment will have the following fields:

- `id`: This is the unique ID for this road segment.
- `name`: This is the name of the road this segment is a part of.
- `centerline`: This is a LineString geometry representing the shape of this road segment.
- `tally`: This is the number of times this road segment was used by the GPS recordings. This is the output of the map matching algorithm we will implement later in this chapter.

Now that we've created the `road_segments` table, we can start implementing the `split_roads.py` program. Create this file and add the following code to it:

```
import psycopg2
import shapely.wkt
import shapely

connection = psycopg2.connect(database="gps_heatmap",
                              user="postgres")
cursor = connection.cursor()

cursor.execute("DELETE FROM road_segments")
```

So far, we have simply opened a connection to the database and deleted any existing road_segments records. As usual, this gives us a blank table where we can store our calculated road segments, removing any segments that we may have stored previously. This allows us to run the program as often as we need.

Next, we want to convert the contents of the roads table into a series of connected road segments. In the previous chapter, we used Shapely to perform this task using road data held in memory. This time, we're going to implement the same process using PostGIS. First, we are going to load a master list of all the road record IDs into memory:

```
all_road_ids = []
cursor.execute("SELECT id FROM roads")
for row in cursor:
    all_road_ids.append(row[0])
```

We will work through each of these roads in turn. For each road, we start by loading the road's name and geometry into memory:

```
for road_id in all_road_ids:
    cursor.execute("SELECT name,ST_AsText(centerline) " +
                   "FROM roads WHERE id=%s", (road_id,))
    name,wkt = cursor.fetchone()
    cur_road = shapely.wkt.loads(wkt)
```

Now that we have got the road's LineString geometry, we want to split it at each point where it touches or crosses another road. To do this, we'll build a list of **crossroads** for this road:

```
crossroads = []
cursor.execute("SELECT ST_AsText(centerline) FROM ROADS" +
               "WHERE ST_Touches(roads.centerline, " +
               "ST_GeomFromText(%s)) OR ST_Crosses(" +
               "roads.centerline, ST_GeomFromText(%s))",
               (wkt, wkt))
for row in cursor:
    crossroad = shapely.wkt.loads(row[0])
    crossroads.append(crossroad)
```

We then use the crossroads to split the current road's geometry into one or more segments:

```
for crossroad in crossroads:
    cur_road = cur_road.difference(crossroad)
```

Next, we need to process the resulting road, dividing it up into a separate LineString for each road segment:

```
segments = []
if cur_road.geom_type == "MultiLineString":
    for segment in cur_road.geoms:
        segments.append(segment)
elif cur_road.geom_type == "LineString":
    segments.append(cur_road)
```

Then, we save the calculated segments into the `road_segments` table:

```
for segment in segments:
    centerline_wkt = shapely.wkt.dumps(segment)
    cursor.execute("INSERT INTO road_segments (name, " +
                   "centerline, tally) VALUES (%s, " +
                   "ST_GeomFromText(%s), %s)",
                   (name, centerline_wkt, 0))
```

Finally (outside the `for road_id in all_road_ids` loop), we commit our changes to the database:

```
connection.commit()
```

This completes our `split_roads.py` program. If you run through the programs in sequence, and then use the `psql` command-line client to access the database, you can see that the program has indeed generated a number of road segments out of the raw road data:

```
% python init_db.py
% python import_roads.py
% python split_roads.py
% psql gps_heatmap
# SELECT count(*) from roads;
1556
# SELECT count(*) from road_segments;
3240
```

As you would expect, there are many more segments than there are roads.

 If you want to view the road segments, you can easily write a program using Mapnik which displays the contents of the `road_segments` table. A version of this program, named `preview_segments.py`, is included in the sample code for this chapter.

Constructing a network of directed road segments

When we try to match the recorded GPS data against a database of road segments, one of the important questions we will need to answer is, "Which other road segments lead off from this one?" To answer this question, we will need to build a **directed network** of road segments.

We did something similar to this in the previous chapter, where we used NetworkX to calculate the shortest path between two points. In this case, however, we are going to store the network in the database for later use.

To make the map matching algorithm easier to implement, our network of road segments will be **directed** — that is, each segment in our road_segments table will actually be represented by two separate road segments:

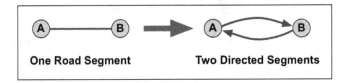

One Road Segment   **Two Directed Segments**

 Of course, not every road is two-way, but we are ignoring this to keep things easier.

As you can see, each road segment is converted into two directed segments: one running from point A to point B, and the other running from point B back to point A.

We are going to use a new table named directed_segments to hold the directed road segments. Each directed segment record will have the following fields:

- id: This is the unique ID for this road segment
- road_segment_id: This is the record ID of the road segment this directed segment is derived from
- centerline: This is the LineString geometry for this directed segment

Note that the directed segment's LineString runs in the same direction as the segment itself — that is, the start of the directed segment is at centerline.coords[0] and the end of the directed segment is at centerline.coords[-1].

A second table, `endpoints`, will hold the coordinates for the ends of the various directed road segments. Each endpoint record will have the following fields:

- `id`: This is the unique ID for this endpoint
- `endpoint`: This is a Point geometry containing the coordinates for this endpoint

 We use a Point geometry here so that we can make spatial queries against this table.

Finally, we are going to need a table that identifies which directed road segments leave from a given endpoint. This table, `endpoint_segments`, will have the following fields:

- `id`: This is the unique ID for this `endpoint_segments` record
- `directed_segment_id`: This is the record ID of a directed road segment
- `endpoint_id`: This is the record ID of the endpoint that this directed road segment leaves from

These three tables will be used to store the network of directed road segments. Let's modify our `init_db.py` program to create these three new tables. To do this, add the following code to the end of this file, immediately before the call to `connection.commit()`:

```
cursor.execute("DROP TABLE IF EXISTS directed_segments")
cursor.execute("CREATE TABLE directed_segments (" +
               "id SERIAL PRIMARY KEY," +
               "road_segment_id INTEGER," +
               "centerline GEOMETRY)")
cursor.execute("CREATE INDEX ON directed_segments USING
GIST(centerline)")

cursor.execute("DROP TABLE IF EXISTS endpoints")
cursor.execute("CREATE TABLE endpoints (" +
               "id SERIAL PRIMARY KEY," +
               "endpoint GEOMETRY)")
cursor.execute("CREATE INDEX ON endpoints USING GIST(endpoint)")

cursor.execute("DROP TABLE IF EXISTS endpoint_segments")
cursor.execute("CREATE TABLE endpoint_segments (" +
               "id SERIAL PRIMARY KEY," +
               "directed_segment_id INTEGER," +
```

```
                        "endpoint_id INTEGER)")
    cursor.execute("CREATE INDEX ON
    endpoint_segments(directed_segment_id)")
    cursor.execute("CREATE INDEX ON endpoint_segments(endpoint_id)")
```

This is the last change we'll need to make to our database structure, so go ahead and re-create the database tables, import the roads, and split them again:

% **python init_db.py**

% **python import_roads.py**

% **python split_roads.py**

 We wouldn't need to rerun our programs each time if we'd used database migrations, but we are keeping the database logic as simple as possible. Fortunately, this is the last time we will need to do this.

We are now ready to calculate the directed road network and store it into the database. The program we will create is called `calc_directed_network.py`; create this file, and enter the following code into it:

```
import networkx
import psycopg2
import shapely.wkt
import shapely.geometry

connection = psycopg2.connect(database="gps_heatmap",
user="postgres")
cursor = connection.cursor()
```

We are now ready to create the NetworkX graph representing the road network. When we did this in the previous chapter, we used the `networkx.read_shp()` function to create a NetworkX `DiGraph` object from the contents of a shapefile. Unfortunately, there's no equivalent function for creating a graph from the contents of a PostGIS database; however, since NetworkX is implemented in Python, it is easy to adapt the source code for the `read_shp()` function to do what we want. Add the following code to the end of your `calc_directed_network.py` program:

```
network = networkx.Graph()

cursor.execute("SELECT id,ST_AsText(centerline) FROM
road_segments")
for row in cursor:
    road_segment_id,wkt = row
```

```
linestring = shapely.wkt.loads(wkt)

first_pt = linestring.coords[0]
last_pt  = linestring.coords[-1]

network.add_edge(first_pt, last_pt,
                    {'road_segment_id' : road_segment_id})
```

The nodes in the NetworkX graph are a (long, lat) tuple identifying each road segment's endpoints, and the edges represent the directed road segments. Note that we store the record ID of the road segment as an attribute in the graph so that we can refer to it later.

Now that we have the NetworkX graph, let's prepare to use it to generate the directed network of connected road segments. To do this, we have to calculate the **largest connected subgraph** from the graph we have built, just like we did in the previous chapter. Here is the necessary code:

```
sub_graphs = list(networkx.connected_component_subgraphs(network))
largest = sub_graphs[0]
```

We now have a graph containing all the connected road segments. We can now use this to store the road segment endpoints into the database:

```
cursor.execute("DELETE FROM endpoints")

endpoint_ids = {}
for node in largest.nodes():
    point = shapely.geometry.Point(node)
    wkt = shapely.wkt.dumps(point)

    cursor.execute("INSERT INTO endpoints (endpoint) " +
                    "VALUES (ST_GeomFromText(%s)) RETURNING id",
                    (wkt,))
    endpoint_id = cursor.fetchone()[0]

    endpoint_ids[node] = endpoint_id
```

Notice that the endpoint_ids dictionary maps a (long, lat) coordinate to the record ID of the endpoint in the database. We will use this to link the directed road segments to their endpoints.

Our final task is to store the directed road segments, along with the endpoint the segment starts from. We'll start by deleting the existing records in the database, and iterating over the road segments in our graph:

```
cursor.execute("DELETE FROM directed_segments")
cursor.execute("DELETE FROM endpoint_segments")

for node1,node2 in largest.edges():
    endpoint_id_1 = endpoint_ids[node1]
    endpoint_id_2 = endpoint_ids[node2]
    road_segment_id = largest.get_edge_data(node1,
        node2)['road_segment_id']

    cursor.execute("SELECT ST_AsText(centerline) " +
                   "FROM road_segments WHERE id=%s",
                   (road_segment_id,))
    wkt = cursor.fetchone()[0]
    linestring = shapely.wkt.loads(wkt)
```

We now have the record ID of the segment's endpoints, and the LineString defining this road segment. We now need to convert this segment into two *directed* segments, one heading in each direction:

```
reversed_coords = list(reversed(linestring.coords))
if node1 == linestring.coords[0]:
    forward_linestring = linestring
    reverse_linestring = shapely.geometry.LineString(reversed_
coords)
else:
    reverse_linestring = linestring
    forward_linestring = shapely.geometry.LineString(reversed_
coords)
```

This gives us two LineString geometries, one running from the first endpoint to the second, and the other running from the second endpoint back to the first. We can now save the information we've calculated into the database:

```
cursor.execute("INSERT INTO directed_segments " +
               "(road_segment_id,centerline) VALUES " +
               "(%s, ST_GeomFromText(%s)) RETURNING id",
               (road_segment_id, forward_linestring.wkt))
forward_segment_id = cursor.fetchone()[0]

cursor.execute("INSERT INTO directed_segments " +
               "(road_segment_id,centerline) VALUES " +
```

```
                        "(%s, ST_GeomFromText(%s)) RETURNING id",
                        (road_segment_id, reverse_linestring.wkt))
        reverse_segment_id = cursor.fetchone()[0]

        cursor.execute("INSERT INTO endpoint_segments " +
                        "(directed_segment_id, endpoint_id) " +

                        "VALUES (%s, %s)",

                        (forward_segment_id, endpoint_id_1))


            cursor.execute("INSERT INTO endpoint_segments " +
                        "(directed_segment_id, endpoint_id) " +

                        "VALUES (%s, %s)",

                        (reverse_segment_id, endpoint_id_2))
```

To finish our program, we have to commit the changes we've made:

```
        connection.commit()
```

You can now create the network of the directed road segments by running this program:

```
% python calc_directed_network.py
```

Implementing the map matching algorithm

We are now ready, at long last, to implement our map matching algorithm. The algorithm we will use is derived from the paper: *Map-matching of GPS traces on high-resolution navigation networks using the Multiple Hypothesis Technique (MHT)*, written by Nadine Schuessler and Kay Axhausen for the Institute of Transport Planning and Systems in Switzerland.

If you are interested in reading this paper, it can be found at www.ivt.ethz.ch/vpl/publications/reports/ab568.pdf. This algorithm is based on the notion of a **route candidate**, which is a possible path the traveler could have taken as the GPS points were recorded. Each route candidate has a list of directed road segments and a **score** identifying how closely the GPS points match those road segments.

The journey is recreated by following the GPS points one at a time. At any particular moment, there is a list of route candidates which could possibly match the GPS coordinates which have been processed thus far. As each new GPS point is processed, the route candidates are updated one at a time by comparing the GPS coordinate with the route candidate's final road segment.

If the GPS point is considered to still be somewhere on that final segment, then the GPS point is simply added to that segment and the route candidate's score is updated. If, on the other hand, the GPS point is beyond the end of the route candidate's final road segment, then we look at the road network to see which other road segments lead off from that point. We then create new route candidates for each road segment leaving from that endpoint:

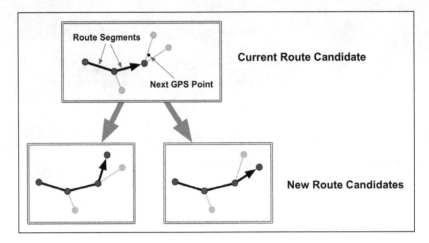

Once all the GPS points have been processed, we select the route candidate with the lowest score as being the one most likely to have been used for this journey.

To implement this algorithm, we are going to use Python dictionaries to represent a **route segment** — that is, a single segment within a route candidate's journey. Each route segment dictionary will have the following entries:

- `directed_segment_id`: This is the record ID of the `directed_segment` which this segment of the route is following

- `linestring`: This is the road segment's centerline, as a Shapely LineString object

- `gps_points`: This is a list of (long,lat) coordinates defining the GPS points which have been assigned to this route segment

- `gps_distances`: This is a list holding the calculated minimum distance between each GPS point and the segment's LineString

Each route candidate is going to be represented by a Python dictionary with the following entries:

- `segments`: This is a list of the route segments that make up this route candidate.

- directed_segment_ids: This is a list containing the record ID of each directed segment used by this route. We use this to quickly discard a new route candidate if another route is using the same sequence of road segments.

- score: This is the calculated score for this route candidate. The score is calculated as the sum of the GPS distances in each route segment—in other words, the lower the score, the more closely the GPS points follow this route.

With this information in mind, let's start implementing the map matcher. Create a new Python program called map_matcher.py, and enter the following into this file:

```
import os
import osgeo.ogr
import shapely.geometry
import shapely.wkt
import psycopg2
import pyproj

gps_tracks = []
for fName in os.listdir("gps-data"):
    if fName.endswith(".gpx"):
        srcFile = osgeo.ogr.Open("gps-data/" + fName)
        layer = srcFile.GetLayerByName("tracks")

        for feature_num in range(layer.GetFeatureCount()):
            feature = layer.GetFeature(feature_num)
            geometry = feature.GetGeometryRef()

            if geometry.GetGeometryName() == "MULTILINESTRING":
                for geom_num in \
                  range(geometry.GetGeometryCount()):
                    wkt = geometry.GetGeometryRef
                      (geom_num).ExportToWkt()
                    gps_tracks.append((fName, wkt))
            elif geometry.GetGeometryName() == "LINESTRING":
                wkt = geometry.ExportToWkt()
                gps_tracks.append((fName, wkt))

connection = psycopg2.connect(database="gps_heatmap",
  user="postgres")
cursor = connection.cursor()
```

As you can see, we import the various libraries we'll need, load the recorded GPS data into memory, and open a connection to our database. Next, we want to reset the `tally` values for our road segments:

```
cursor.execute("UPDATE road_segments SET tally=0")
connection.commit()
```

We are now ready to start processing the recorded GPS data. While the paper this algorithm is based on uses a sophisticated process of splitting the GPS data into trip segments, processing each trip segment and then joining the resulting routes together, we are going to use a much simpler approach; we will assume that each GPS recording has no gaps in it, but that it might start or finish away from a road. To handle this, we trim the start and end coordinates until we reach a point within 10 meters of a road.

Add the following to the end of your program:

```
for fName,track_wkt in gps_tracks:
    print "Processing " + fName

    gps_track  = shapely.wkt.loads(track_wkt)
    gps_points = list(gps_track.coords)

    while len(gps_points) > 0:
        circle = calc_circle_with_radius(gps_points[0], 10)
        cursor.execute("SELECT count(*) FROM road_segments " +
                "WHERE ST_Intersects(ST_GeomFromText(%s)," +
                        "centerline)", (circle.wkt,))
        if cursor.fetchone()[0] == 0:
            del gps_points[0]
        else:
            break

    while len(gps_points) > 0:
        circle = calc_circle_with_radius(gps_points[-1], 10)
        cursor.execute("SELECT count(*) FROM road_segments " +
                "WHERE ST_Intersects(ST_GeomFromText(%s)," +
                        "centerline)", (circle.wkt,))
        if cursor.fetchone()[0] == 0:
            del gps_points[-1]
        else:
            break
```

We are simply processing each GPS track in turn, trimming points from the start and end until we find a GPS point which is within 10 meters of a road segment. Notice that we're using a function named `calc_circle_with_radius()` to create a Shapely polygon that describes a circle 10 meters around a GPS coordinate, and then ask the database to find any road segments within that circle. Let's go ahead and implement that `calc_circle_with_radius()` function; place this at the top of your program, immediately after the `import` statements:

```
def calc_circle_with_radius(center_point, radius):
    geod = pyproj.Geod(ellps="WGS84")
    sLong,sLat = center_point
    eLong,eLat,iHeading = geod.fwd(sLong, sLat, 0, radius)
    lat_delta = abs(sLat - eLat)
    return shapely.geometry.Point(sLong, sLat).buffer(lat_delta)
```

Now that we have the set of relevant GPS points within each recording, we are ready to start map matching. The first step is to build an initial set of route candidates based on the starting GPS point. We do this by identifying all road endpoints within 750 meters of the GPS point, and create a (single-segment) route candidate for each road segment leading off from those endpoints. Following Schuessler and Axhausen's paper, we ensure that there are at least 25 route candidates, and if there are not, we expand the search area by 100 meters and try again.

Add the following code to the end of your program:

```
search_distance = 750
while True:
    circle = calc_circle_with_radius(gps_points[0],
                                     search_distance)

    cursor.execute("SELECT id FROM endpoints " +
                   "WHERE ST_Contains(ST_GeomFromText(%s)," +
                   "endpoint)", (circle.wkt,))
    possible_endpoints = []
    for row in cursor:
        possible_endpoints.append(row[0])

    possible_road_segments = []
    for endpoint_id in possible_endpoints:
        cursor.execute("SELECT directed_segment_id " +
                       "FROM endpoint_segments " +
                       "WHERE endpoint_id=%s", (endpoint_id,))
        for row in cursor:
            directed_segment_id = row[0]
```

```
                    possible_road_segments.append(
                        (directed_segment_id, endpoint_id))

        route_candidates = []
        for directed_segment_id,endpoint_id in
            possible_road_segments:
            cursor.execute("SELECT ST_AsText(centerline) " +
                        "FROM directed_segments WHERE id=%s",
                        (directed_segment_id,))
            wkt = cursor.fetchone()[0]
            linestring = shapely.wkt.loads(wkt)
            gps_distance = calc_distance(gps_points[0],
                                    linestring)

            segment = {
                'directed_segment_id' : directed_segment_id,
                'linestring' : linestring,
                'gps_points': [gps_points[0]],
                'gps_distances': [gps_distance] }
            route_segments = [segment]

            candidate = {
                'segments': route_segments,
                'directed_segment_ids' : [directed_segment_id],
                'score': calc_score(route_segments) }
            route_candidates.append(candidate)

        if len(route_candidates) >= 25:
            break
        else:
            search_distance = search_distance + 100
            continue
```

As you can see, we create a single route segment dictionary and a route
candidate dictionary for each possible route candidate, storing the results in
the `route_candidates` list. There are two more functions that we need here:
one to calculate the distance from a given point to the closest point within a given
Shapely geometry, and another to calculate the score for a given route candidate.
Go ahead and add these two functions to the top of your program:

```
def calc_distance(point, geometry):
    return shapely.geometry.Point(point).distance(geometry)

def calc_score(route_segments):
    total = 0
```

```
    for segment in route_segments:
        total = total + sum(segment['gps_distances'])

    return total
```

Now that we have an initial set of route candidates, we have to **develop** them by adding each successive GPS point to each route candidate, generating new route candidates as we reach the end of each road segment. At the same time, we **trim** the list of route candidates to stop it from growing too large.

The bulk of our work will be done in a function named `develop_route()`. This function will take a route candidate and a GPS point (as well as a few other parameters), and return a list of new or updated route candidates to include for processing in the next iteration. Let's write the code which uses this function; add the following to the end of your program:

```
    for next_point in gps_points[1:]:
        num_routes_to_process = len(route_candidates)
        for i in range(num_routes_to_process):
            route = route_candidates.pop(0)
            new_candidates = develop_route(next_point, route,
                route_candidates, cursor)
            route_candidates.extend(new_candidates)
```

We process each route candidate exactly once, first removing it from the list of candidates using `route_candidates.pop(0)`, and then passing the candidate to the `develop_route()` function. We then add the new or updated route candidates to the end of the `route_candidates` list. By the time our `for i in range(num_routes_to_process)` loop has finished, we would have processed each route candidate exactly once, either incorporating the GPS point into that route candidate or replacing it with a new set of route candidates.

Before we start processing the next GPS point, we need to trim the list of route candidates. According to Schuessler and Axhausen, a highly effective way of doing this is to repeatedly remove the route candidate with the highest score until there are no more than 40 remaining candidates. Let's do this now:

```
        while len(route_candidates) > 40:
            highest = None
            for index,route in enumerate(route_candidates):
                if highest == None:
                    highest = index
                elif route['score'] >
                  route_candidates[highest]['score']:
                    highest = index
            del route_candidates[highest]
```

[Make sure you put this code inside the `for next_point in...` loop.]

Before we implement the `develop_route()` function, let's finish writing the main part of our program. We have now processed all the GPS points, so we can check the score for each remaining route candidate and choose the candidate with the lowest score (excluding any candidates with fewer than two route segments). This is the route candidate most likely to have been taken by the GPS points. We then increment the tally for each road segment used by that route. Here is the relevant code:

```
best_route = None
for route in route_candidates:
    if len(route['segments']) >= 2:
        if best_route == None:
            best_route = route
        elif route['score'] < best_route['score']:
            best_route = route

if best_route == None: continue

for segment in best_route['segments']:
    cursor.execute("SELECT road_segment_id " +
                   "FROM directed_segments WHERE id=%s",
                   (segment['directed_segment_id'],))
    road_segment_id = cursor.fetchone()[0]
    cursor.execute("UPDATE road_segments SET tally=tally+1" +
                   "WHERE id=%s", (road_segment_id,))

connection.commit()
```

We now need to implement the `develop_route()` function. This function uses the following logic, taken from the paper by Schuessler and Axhausen:

1. If the route candidate has only one segment, see whether the GPS point has reached the start of that segment's LineString. If this happens, the GPS recording must be following the directed road segment in the wrong direction, so we discard the route candidate.

2. See whether the GPS point is still within the route candidate's final segment. If so, add the GPS point to that final segment, recalculate the candidate's score, and return it for further processing.

3. If the GPS point is beyond the end of the route candidate's final segment, identify the endpoint we have reached and create a new route candidate for each directed road segment leaving from that endpoint. We check the validity of each of the new route candidates, and return the valid candidates for further processing.

Let's start implementing this function:

```
def develop_route(next_point, route, route_candidates, cursor):
    if len(route['segments']) == 1:
        if point_at_start_of_segment(next_point,
                                     route['segments'][0]):
            return []

    last_segment = route['segments'][-1]

    if point_in_route_segment(next_point, last_segment):
        next_distance = calc_distance(next_point,
                                      last_segment['linestring'])
        last_segment['gps_points'].append(next_point)
        last_segment['gps_distances'].append(next_distance)
        route['score'] = calc_score(route['segments'])
        return [route]
```

This implements the first two of the steps described earlier. Notice that we use a couple of new functions, `point_at_start_of_segment()` and `point_in_route_segment()`, to do all the hard work. We'll implement these functions shortly, but first let's work through the process of creating a new set of route candidates once the GPS point has gone past the end of the last route segment.

The first step in this process is to identify the current endpoint that we have reached. Add the following to the end of your `develop_route()` function:

```
last_point = last_segment['linestring'].coords[-1]
endpoint = shapely.geometry.Point(last_point)

cursor.execute("SELECT id FROM endpoints " +
               "WHERE endpoint=ST_GeomFromText(%s)",
               (endpoint.wkt,))
endpoint_id = cursor.fetchone()[0]
```

Next, we will build a list of all the directed road segments that leave from this endpoint:

```
possible_segment_ids = []
cursor.execute("SELECT directed_segment_id " +
               "FROM endpoint_segments " +
               "WHERE endpoint_id=%s", (endpoint_id,))
for row in cursor:
    possible_segment_ids.append(row[0])
```

We now need to create a new route candidate for each of the possible road segments. For each route candidate, we create a single route segment using that directed road segment:

```
new_candidates = []
for directed_segment_id in possible_segment_ids:
    cursor.execute("SELECT road_segment_id," +
                   "ST_AsText(centerline) " +
                   "FROM directed_segments " +
                   "WHERE id=%s", (directed_segment_id,))
    road_segment_id,wkt = cursor.fetchone()
    linestring = shapely.wkt.loads(wkt)

    next_distance = calc_distance(next_point, linestring)

    new_segment = {}
    new_segment['directed_segment_id'] = directed_segment_id
    new_segment['linestring'] = linestring
    new_segment['gps_points'] = [next_point]
    new_segment['gps_distances'] = [next_distance]

    new_candidate = {}
    new_candidate['segments'] = []
    new_candidate['segments'].extend(route['segments'])
    new_candidate['segments'].append(new_segment)
    new_candidate['directed_segment_ids'] = []
    new_candidate['directed_segment_ids'].extend(
                        route['directed_segment_ids'])
```

```
            new_candidate['directed_segment_ids'].append(directed_segment_
   id)

            if not route_is_valid(new_candidate, route_candidates,
                                  new_candidates):
                continue

            new_candidate['score'] =
                calc_score(new_candidate['segments'])
            new_candidates.append(new_candidate)
        return new_candidates
```

Notice that we check the new route's validity using another function, `route_is_valid()`. We will also have to implement this function.

This completes the `develop_route()` function itself. Let's now write the `point_at_start_of_segment()` function, which determines whether the GPS track is running the wrong way along a directed road segment:

```
def point_at_start_of_segment(next_point, segment):
    num_points = len(segment['gps_points'])
    if num_points > 0:
        average_distance = sum(segment['gps_distances']) /
            num_points

        startpoint_coord = segment['linestring'].coords[0]
        startpoint = shapely.geometry.Point(startpoint_coord)
        endpoint_coord = segment['linestring'].coords[-1]
        endpoint = shapely.geometry.Point(endpoint_coord)

        distance_to_start = calc_distance(next_point, startpoint)
        distance_to_end   = calc_distance(next_point, endpoint)

        if distance_to_start < 2 * average_distance:
            if distance_to_end > 2 * average_distance:
                return True
    return False
```

This code is a bit of a kludge, comparing the distance from the current point to the road segment's start and endpoints, but it works well enough for our purposes.

Next, we need to implement the `point_in_route_segment()` function. We will use two separate tests to see whether the point has reached the segment's endpoint. First off, we know we have reached the endpoint if the distance from the GPS point to the closest point on the segment's LineString is equal to the distance from the point to the end of that LineString:

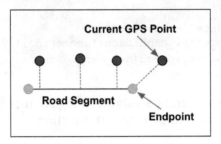

Here is the first part of the `point_in_route_segment()` function, which implements this test:

```
def point_in_route_segment(point, segment):
    endpoint =
        shapely.geometry.Point(segment['linestring'].coords[-1])

    distance_to_linestring = calc_distance(point,
                                       segment['linestring'])
    distance_to_endpoint = calc_distance(point, endpoint)

    if distance_to_linestring == distance_to_endpoint:
        return False
```

The second test involves comparing the length of the final route segment with the length of a LineString built out of the GPS points assigned to that route segment. If the GPS LineString is longer than the road segment, then we must have reached the end of that segment:

```
    gps_coords = []
    gps_coords.extend(segment['gps_points'])
    gps_coords.append(point)

    gps_length = shapely.geometry.LineString(gps_coords).length
    segment_length = segment['linestring'].length

    if gps_length > segment_length:
        return False
```

Finally, if the GPS point failed both of these tests, then it must still be within the current route segment:

```
return True
```

 The paper by Schuessler and Axhausen suggests a third test, comparing the direction of the GPS track against the direction of the road segment. However, it was not clear how this could be implemented where road segments are complex LineStrings rather than straight line segments, so we won't use this test in our implementation of the map matching algorithm.

This completes the `point_in_route_segment()` function. The last function we need to implement is `route_is_valid()`. A route candidate is considered to be valid if:

1. It is unique; that is, there is no other route candidate with the exact same sequence of road segments

2. Its final road segment does not go back to the start of the previous segment; that is, the route doesn't double back on itself.

3. The route doesn't include the same directed road segment twice

In order to calculate uniqueness, the `route_is_valid()` function will need not only a list of all the current route candidates, but also a list of the new candidates being created by the `develop_route()` function. For this reason, the `route_is_valid()` function accepts both the current list of route candidates and the list of new candidates being created.

Here is the first part of the implementation of this function, including the uniqueness check:

```
def route_is_valid(route, route_candidates, new_candidates):
    route_roads = route['directed_segment_ids']

    for other_route in route_candidates:
        if route_roads == other_route['directed_segment_ids']:
            return False

    for other_route in new_candidates:
        if route_roads == other_route['directed_segment_ids']:
            return False
```

The following code checks that a route does not double back on itself:

```
if len(route['segments']) >= 2:
    last_segment = route['segments'][-1]
    prev_segment = route['segments'][-2]

    last_segment_end   = last_segment['linestring'].coords[-1]
    prev_segment_start = prev_segment['linestring'].coords[0]

    if last_segment_end == prev_segment_start:
        return False
```

Finally, we ensure that the same directed road segment isn't being used twice:

```
directed_segment_ids = set()
for segment in route['segments']:
    directed_segment_id = segment['directed_segment_id']
    if directed_segment_id in directed_segment_ids:
        return False
    else:
        directed_segment_ids.add(directed_segment_id)
```

If the route passes all three checks, then it is considered to be valid:

```
return True
```

This completes the implementation of the `route_is_valid()` function, and indeed the implementation of the entire `map_matcher.py` program. You should be able to run it from the command line and see each GPS recording being processed in turn:

```
% python map_matcher.py
Processing ride_2015_01_08.gpx
Processing ride_2015_01_11.gpx
Processing ride_2015_01_23.gpx
...
```

Because there are thousands of points in each GPS recording, the program will take a few minutes to process each file. Once it has finished, the `tally` field in the `road_segments` table would have been updated to show the number of times each road segment was used. You can check this using the Postgres command-line client:

```
% psql gps_heatmap
# SELECT name,tally FROM road_segments WHERE tally > 0 ORDER BY tally
DESC;
```

3560	otonga rd	42
6344	wychwood cres	42
3561	otonga rd	42
3557	otonga rd	42
3558	otonga rd	42
3559	otonga rd	42
6343	wychwood cres	41
6246	springfield rd	19
6300	old taupo rd	19

As you can see, map matching is quite a complex process, but this program actually works pretty well. Now that we've calculated the tallies, we can write the final part of our GPS Heatmap system: the program that displays the heatmap based on the calculated tally values.

Generating the GPS heatmap

We are going to use Mapnik to generate the heatmap, creating a separate mapnik.Rule for each unique tally value so that the color used for each road segment varies depending on its tally. This program will be called generate_heatmap.py; create this program and enter the following code into it:

```
import mapnik
import psycopg2

MAX_WIDTH = 1200
MAX_HEIGHT = 800
MIN_TALLY = 3

connection = psycopg2.connect(database="gps_heatmap",
                              user="postgres")
cursor = connection.cursor()
```

After importing the libraries we need and defining some constants, we open up a connection to the database so that we can calculate the highest tally value and the bounds of the calculated heatmap. Let's do that now:

```
cursor.execute("SELECT max(tally) FROM road_segments")
max_tally = cursor.fetchone()[0]

cursor.execute("SELECT ST_XMIN(ST_EXTENT(centerline)), " +
               "ST_YMIN(ST_EXTENT(centerline)), " +
```

```
        "ST_XMAX(ST_EXTENT(centerline)), " +
        "ST_YMAX(ST_EXTENT(centerline)) " +
        "FROM road_segments WHERE tally >= %s" % MIN_TALLY)
min_long,min_lat,max_long,max_lat = cursor.fetchone()
```

As you can see, we use the MIN_TALLY constant to zoom in on the more popular parts of the heatmap. You can change this value if you want; setting it to 1 will display every road segment covered by a GPS track, and setting it to a higher value will focus in on the most commonly used portions of the map.

Now that we know the area of the Earth covered by the heatmap, we can calculate the dimensions of the map image. We want to use the specified maximum size, while maintaining the aspect ratio of the map:

```
extent = mapnik.Envelope(min_long, min_lat,  max_long, max_lat)
aspectRatio = extent.width() / extent.height()

mapWidth = MAX_WIDTH
mapHeight = int(mapWidth / aspectRatio)
if mapHeight > MAX_HEIGHT:
    scaleFactor = float(MAX_HEIGHT) / float(mapHeight)
    mapWidth = int(mapWidth * scaleFactor)
    mapHeight = int(mapHeight * scaleFactor)
```

Next, we initialize the map itself:

```
map = mapnik.Map(mapWidth, mapHeight)
map.background = mapnik.Color("white")
```

Even though only some of the road segments would have been used by the GPS recordings, we still want to show all the unused road segments as a backdrop for the heatmap. To do this, we will create an unused_roads layer and corresponding Mapnik style:

```
layer = mapnik.Layer("unused_roads")
layer.datasource = mapnik.PostGIS(host='localhost',
                                  user='postgres',
                                  password='',
                                  dbname='gps_heatmap',
                                  table='road_segments')
layer.styles.append("unused_road_style")
map.layers.append(layer)

line_symbol = mapnik.LineSymbolizer(mapnik.Color("#c0c0c0"), 1.0)

rule = mapnik.Rule()
```

```
rule.filter = mapnik.Filter("[tally] = 0")
rule.symbols.append(line_symbol)

style = mapnik.Style()
style.rules.append(rule)
map.append_style("unused_road_style", style)
```

Notice that we use a `mapnik.PostGIS()` datasource so that the map layer takes its data directly from our PostGIS database.

Next, we need to define a map layer for the roads which were used (that is, the roads which have a `tally` value of 1 or more). This map layer, which we will call `used_roads`, will have a separate `mapnik.Rule()` for each unique tally value. This allows us to assign a different color to each unique tally value so that the color used for each road segment varies according to that segment's tally. To implement this, we will need a function that calculates the `mapnik.Stroke()` to use for a given tally value. Here is that function, which you should place near the top of your program:

```
def calc_stroke(value, max_value):
    fraction = float(value) / float(max_value)

    def interpolate(start_value, end_value, fraction):
        return start_value + (end_value - start_value) * fraction

    r = interpolate(0.7, 0.0, fraction)
    g = interpolate(0.7, 0.0, fraction)
    b = interpolate(1.0, 0.4, fraction)

    color = mapnik.Color(int(r*255), int(g*255), int(b*255))
    width = max(4.0 * fraction, 1.5)

    return mapnik.Stroke(color, width)
```

The `interpolate()` helper function is used to calculate a color range from pale blue to dark blue. We also adjust the width of the displayed road segment according to the tally so that more frequently used roads are drawn with a wider stroke on the map.

If you want, you can change the starting and ending colors to make the heatmap more colorful. As mentioned earlier, we are just using shades of blue so that the heatmap makes sense when printed in black and white.

With this function implemented, we can add the `used_roads` layer to our map. To do this, add the following code to the end of your program:

```
layer = mapnik.Layer("used_roads")
layer.datasource = mapnik.PostGIS(host='localhost',
                                  user='postgres',
                                  password='',
                                  dbname='gps_heatmap',
                                  table='road_segments')
layer.styles.append("used_road_style")
map.layers.append(layer)

style = mapnik.Style()
for tally in range(1, max_tally+1):
    line_symbol = mapnik.LineSymbolizer()
    line_symbol.stroke = calc_stroke(tally, max_tally)

    rule = mapnik.Rule()
    rule.filter = mapnik.Filter("[tally] = %d" % tally)
    rule.symbols.append(line_symbol)

    style.rules.append(rule)
map.append_style("used_road_style", style)
```

Finally, we can render the map, saving the results to an image file on the disk:

```
map.zoom_to_box(extent)
mapnik.render_to_file(map, "heatmap.png", "png")
```

After running this program, you should get a `heatmap.png` file containing the generated heatmap:

Congratulations! This program is anything but trivial, and solves a number of geospatial problems along the way in producing this image. Of course, you can use this program to match your own GPS recordings against a road network, but what we have really done is shown how complex geospatial problems can be solved one step at a time, using the various techniques described throughout this book.

Further improvements

While the GPS Heatmap system works surprisingly well, it is not perfect. No program is ever complete. If you're inclined, you might want to consider the following:

- Make the road-segmentation algorithm more sophisticated to support one-way roads, and points where two roads intersect but do not join (for example, on a highway overpass).

- Improve the route-development process to allow it to capture routes that include U-turns and repeated road segments.

- Take the raw GPS data and split it into contiguous segments, process each segment in turn, and then join the processed segments back together again. This will allow the algorithm to work with GPS recordings that include gaps in the recorded data.

- Combine the map matching algorithm with a shortest-path calculation to write your own turn-by-turn navigation system.

- Look at ways to improve the speed of the map matching algorithm. For example, if two different route candidates use the same road segment, those two candidates should be able to share the calculated distance between a point and that road segment. This will avoid having to calculate the same distance twice. There are bound to be other ways you could optimize the map matcher so that it runs even faster.

- Add a nice-looking raster basemap image to the generated heatmap.

Summary

Congratulations! You have finished implementing a suite of programs that use a range of geospatial analysis techniques to match recorded GPS data to an existing network of roads. In the process of creating the GPS Heatmap system, you have learned how to convert existing road data into a network, how to represent a network of roads within a database, and how to use this data to implement a sophisticated map matching algorithm. This algorithm was then used to calculate a tally of how often each road segment was used by the recorded GPS data, and the tallies were then used to generate a nice-looking heatmap showing the most commonly used roads.

Even if you are not interested in capturing your own GPS data and matching it against a map, the techniques we have used in this chapter will give you many ideas for your own development efforts. Using a combination of Python, GDAL and OGR, Shapely, PyProj, PostGIS and Mapnik, you now have a fantastic arsenal of tools for processing, analyzing and displaying geospatial data. To learn more, check out the following references:

- `http://gdal.org` is the main website for the GDAL and OGR libraries.

- `http://trac.osgeo.org/gdal/wiki/GdalOgrInPython` describes the overall design of the Python interface to GDAL and OGR.

- `http://trac.osgeo.org/gdal/wiki/PythonGotchas` lists a number of issues to be aware of when using GDAL/OGR from Python.

- `http://pypi.python.org/pypi/Shapely` is the main website for the Shapely library.

- `http://toblerity.org/shapely/manual.html` is where you can find the Shapely user manual.

- `https://trac.osgeo.org/proj` describes the Proj.4 cartographic projection library.

- `http://jswhit.github.io/pyproj` is the main site for the Python interface to the Proj library.

- `http://www.postgresql.org` is the main site for the PostgreSQL database.

- `http://postgis.net` is the site for the PostGIS extension to Postgres.

- `http://mapnik.org` is the main site for the Mapnik library.

- Finally, `http://github.com/mapnik/mapnik/wiki` provides a lot of useful information to help you work with Mapnik.

This particular book is now finished, but I hope I have left you with a greater understanding of the tools and techniques you can use for geospatial analysis, and how Python can be used as the foundation for your own geospatial development efforts. The rest is up to you.

Index

J

JavaScript Object Notation (JSON) 27

K

KML (Keyhole Markup Language) 5
koordinates
  reference link 138

L

Landsat satellites
  URL 32
layers 38
lengths
  calculating 116-120
libraries, spatial analysis
  about 106
  NetworkX 111, 112
  PyProj 106-110
Linear Ring 53
line placement 94
lines 4
LineString 53
LineSymbolizer
  about 91
  URL, for documentation 92

M

map
  building 84, 85
  GPS data, matching against 134
  styling 85-87
map layers 81
map matching 134
Mapnik
  about 79
  exploring 80-83
  installing 80
  map, building 84, 85
  map, styling 85-87
  URL 79
  working 87
map object 81
map rendering 97
metadata 3

multiband raster files 31
MultiPolygon 54

N

National Elevation Dataset
  URL 37
National Geospatial Intelligence
    Service (NGIS) 20
Natural Earth Data
  about 33
  URL 33
necessary data
  obtaining 136
neighboring countries program
  example 14-16
NetworkX
  about 106, 111
  references 112
no-data value 30
nodes 111
NumPy
  about 41
  URL 41

O

OGR installer
  URL 7
ogr plugin
  about 88
  URL, for documentation 88
Open Geospatial Consortium (OGC) 29
OpenSourceGeospatialFoundation 6
OpenStreetMap
  about 34
  URL 34
OSGeo installer
  URL 7
osm plugin
  about 88
  URL, for documentation 88

P

physical data 33
pip
  URL, for installing 8

About Packt Publishing

Packt, pronounced 'packed', published its first book, *Mastering phpMyAdmin for Effective MySQL Management*, in April 2004, and subsequently continued to specialize in publishing highly focused books on specific technologies and solutions.

Our books and publications share the experiences of your fellow IT professionals in adapting and customizing today's systems, applications, and frameworks. Our solution-based books give you the knowledge and power to customize the software and technologies you're using to get the job done. Packt books are more specific and less general than the IT books you have seen in the past. Our unique business model allows us to bring you more focused information, giving you more of what you need to know, and less of what you don't.

Packt is a modern yet unique publishing company that focuses on producing quality, cutting-edge books for communities of developers, administrators, and newbies alike. For more information, please visit our website at www.packtpub.com.

About Packt Open Source

In 2010, Packt launched two new brands, Packt Open Source and Packt Enterprise, in order to continue its focus on specialization. This book is part of the Packt Open Source brand, home to books published on software built around open source licenses, and offering information to anybody from advanced developers to budding web designers. The Open Source brand also runs Packt's Open Source Royalty Scheme, by which Packt gives a royalty to each open source project about whose software a book is sold.

Writing for Packt

We welcome all inquiries from people who are interested in authoring. Book proposals should be sent to author@packtpub.com. If your book idea is still at an early stage and you would like to discuss it first before writing a formal book proposal, then please contact us; one of our commissioning editors will get in touch with you.

We're not just looking for published authors; if you have strong technical skills but no writing experience, our experienced editors can help you develop a writing career, or simply get some additional reward for your expertise.

QGIS Python Programming Cookbook

ISBN: 978-1-78398-498-5   Paperback: 340 pages

Over 140 recipes to help you turn QGIS from a desktop GIS tool into a powerful automated geospatial framework

1. Use Python and QGIS to create and transform data, produce appealing GIS visualizations, and build complex map layouts.

2. Learn undocumented features of the new QGIS processing module.

3. A set of user-friendly recipes that can automate the entire geospatial workflows by connecting Python GIS building blocks into comprehensive processes.

Learning R for Geospatial Analysis

ISBN: 978-1-78398-436-7   Paperback: 364 pages

Leverage the power of R to elegantly manage crucial geospatial analysis tasks

1. Write powerful R scripts to manipulate your spatial data.

2. Gain insight from spatial patterns utilizing R's advanced computation and visualization capabilities.

3. Work within a single spatial analysis environment from start to finish.

Please check **www.PacktPub.com** for information on our titles

Learning Geospatial Analysis with Python

ISBN: 978-1-78328-113-8   Paperback: 364 pages

Master GIS and Remote Sensing analysis using Python with these easy to follow tutorials

1. Construct applications for GIS development by exploiting Python.

2. Focuses on built-in Python modules and libraries compatible with the Python Packaging Index distribution system – no compiling of C libraries necessary.

3. This is a practical, hands-on tutorial that teaches you all about Geospatial analysis in Python.

Python Geospatial Development
Second Edition

ISBN: 978-1-78216-152-3   Paperback: 508 pages

Learn to build sophisticated mapping applications from scratch using Python tools for geospatial development

1. Build your own complete and sophisticated mapping applications in Python.

2. Walks you through the process of building your own online system for viewing and editing geospatial data.

3. Practical, hands-on tutorial that teaches you all about geospatial development in Python.

Please check **www.PacktPub.com** for information on our titles

www.ingramcontent.com/pod-product-compliance
Lightning Source LLC
Chambersburg PA
CBHW060128060326
40690CB00018B/3792